Arnold Henry Savage Landor

In the forbidden land

an account of a journey into Tibet, capture by the Tibetan lamas and soldiers,

imprisonment, torture and ultimate release brought about by Dr. Wilson and the

political peshkar, Karak Sing-Pal

Arnold Henry Savage Landor

In the forbidden land

an account of a journey into Tibet, capture by the Tibetan lamas and soldiers, imprisonment, torture and ultimate release brought about by Dr. Wilson and the political peshkar, Karak Sing-Pal

ISBN/EAN: 9783742847836

Manufactured in Europe, USA, Canada, Australia, Japa

Cover: Foto ©Lupo / pixelio.de

Manufactured and distributed by brebook publishing software (www.brebook.com)

Arnold Henry Savage Landor

In the forbidden land

In the Forbidden Land

*An Account of a Journey into Tibet
Capture by the Tibetan Lamas and
Soldiers, Imprisonment, Torture
and Ultimate Release brought
about by Dr. Wilson and
the Political Peshkar
Karak Sing-Pal*

By A. HENRY SAVAGE LANDOR

WITH THE GOVERNMENT ENQUIRY AND REPORT
AND OTHER OFFICIAL DOCUMENTS BY
J. LARKIN, ESQ., DEPUTED BY THE
GOVERNMENT OF INDIA

*With 1 Photogravure, 8 Colored Plates, 50 Full-page and about
150 Text Illustrations, and a Map from Surveys by the Author*

IN TWO VOLUMES

VOL. II.

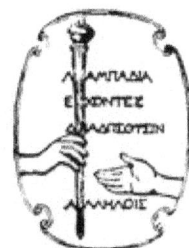

HARPER & BROTHERS PUBLISHERS
NEW YORK AND LONDON
1899

CONTENTS

iii

CONTENTS

CONTENTS

v

CONTENTS

CONTENTS

vii

ILLUSTRATIONS

ix

ILLUSTRATIONS

ILLUSTRATIONS

ILLUSTRATIONS

IN THE FORBIDDEN LAND

IN THE FORBIDDEN LAND

CHAPTER LI

THE START WITH A FURTHER REDUCED PARTY—A RECONNAISSANCE—
NATURAL FORTRESS—BLACK TENTS AND ANIMALS—ON THE WRONG
TACK—SLINGS AND THEIR USE—A VISIT TO A TIBETAN CAMP—MIS-
TAKEN FOR BRIGANDS—BARGAINING AND BEGGING

ALL was promising well when, with my reduced party,
I started towards the northeast, first following for three
and a quarter miles a course of 49°,* skirting the lake,
then ascending over the barren hill ranges in a direction
of 90° for a distance of twelve miles. The journey was un-
eventful, and my four men seemed in the best of spirits.
We descended to a plain where water and grass could be
found, and having seen a camping-ground with a pro-
tecting wall, such as are usually put up by Tibetans at
their halting-places, we made ourselves comfortable for
the night, notwithstanding the high wind and a passing
storm of hail and rain, which drenched us to the skin.
The thermometer during the night went down to 34°.

At sunrise I started to make a reconnaissance from
the top of a high hill wherefrom I could get a bird's-eye
view of a great portion of the surrounding country. It
was of the utmost importance for me to find out which

---

* All bearings given are magnetic.

would be the easiest way to get through the intricate succession of hills and mountains, and to discover the exact direction of a large river to the north of us, throwing itself into the Mansarowar, the name of which no one could tell me. I started alone towards 352° 30' (b. m.), and three and a half miles' climb brought me to 16,480 feet on the summit of a hill, where I was able to ascertain and note down all that I wished to know. I returned to camp, and we went on towards 73° 30', crossing over a pass 16,450 feet, and ultimately finding ourselves at the foot of a hill, the summit of which resembled a fortress, with flying-prayers flapping to and fro in the wind. At the foot of the hill were some twenty ponies grazing.

With the aid of my telescope I was able to make sure that what at first appeared to be a castle was nothing but a work of nature, and that apparently no one was concealed up there. The ponies, however, indicated the presence of men, and we had to move cautiously. In fact, rounding the next hill, we discerned in the grassy valley below a number of black tents, two hundred yaks, and about a thousand sheep. We kept well out of sight behind the hill, and making a long détour, we at last descended to an extensive valley, in which the river described a semicircle, washing the southern hill ranges, where it was joined by a tributary coming from the southeast. This tributary at first appeared to me larger than what I afterwards recognized to be the main stream, so that I followed its course for four miles (92° 30' b. m.), till I found that it was taking me in a more southerly direction than I wished, and had to retrace my steps along a flattish plateau. Meeting two Tibetan women, I purchased, after endless trouble, a fat sheep out of a flock they were driving before them. These two females car-

A NATURAL CASTLE

ried rope slings in their hands, and the accuracy with which they could fling stones and hit the mark at very great distances was really marvellous. For the sake of a few annas they gave an exhibition of their skill, hitting any sheep you pointed at in their flock, even at distances of thirty and forty yards. I tried to obtain from these dangerous females a little information about the country, but they professed absolute ignorance.

"We are menials," they said, "and we know nothing. We know each sheep in our flock, and that is all, but our lord, of whom we are the slaves, knows all. He knows where the rivers come from, and the ways to all Gombas. He is a great king."

"And where does he live?" I inquired.

"There, two miles off, where that smoke rises to the sky."

The temptation was great to go and call on this "great king," who knew so many things, all the more so as we might probably persuade him to sell us provisions, which, as we had none too many, would be of great assistance to us. Anyhow the visit would be interesting, and I decided to risk it.

SLING

We steered towards the several columns of smoke that rose before us, and eventually we approach a large camp of black tents. Our appearance caused a good deal of commotion, and men and women rushed in and out of their tents in great excitement.

"*Jogpas! Jogpas!*" (Brigands! Brigands!) somebody in their camp shouted, and in a moment their matchlocks were made ready, and the few men who had remained outside the tents drew their swords, holding them clumsily in their hands in a way hardly likely to terrify any one.

To be taken for brigands was a novel experience for us, and the warlike array was in strange contrast to the terrified expressions on the faces of those who stood there armed. In fact, when Chanden Sing and I walked forward and encouraged them to sheathe their steels and put their matchlocks by, they readily followed our advice, and brought out rugs for us to sit upon. Having overcome their fright, they were now most anxious to be pleasant.

"*Kiula gunge gozai deva labodu*" (You have nice clothes). I began the conversation, attempting flattery, to put the chieftain at his ease.

WOMAN CARRYING CHILD
IN BASKET

"*Lasso, leh*" (Yes, sir), answered the Tibetan, apparently astonished, and looking at his own attire with an air of comical pride.

His answer was sufficient to show me that the man considered me his superior, the affirmative in Tibetan to an equal or inferior being the mere word *lasso* without the *leh*.

"*Kiula tuku taka zando?*" (How many children have you?) I rejoined.

"*Ni*" (Two).

"*Chuwen bogpe, tsamba, chou won i?*" (Will you sell me flour or *tsamba*?)

"*Middu*" (Have not got any), he replied, making several quick semicircular movements with the upturned palm of his right hand.

This is a most characteristic action of the Tibetan, and nearly invariably accompanies the word "No," instead of a movement of the head, as with us.

4

"*Keran ga Naddoung?*" (Where are you going?) he asked me, eagerly.

"*Nhgarang ne Koroun!*" (I am a pilgrim!) "*Lungba quorghen neh jelghen.*" (I go looking at sacred places.) "*Gopria zaldo. Chakzal wortzic. Tsamba middu. Bogpe middu, guram middu, dic middu, kassar middu.*" (I am very poor. Please hear me. I have no *tsamba*, no flour, no sweet paste, no rice, no dried fruit.)

This, of course, I knew to be untrue, so I calmly said that I would remain seated where I was until food was sold to me, and at the same time produced one or two silver coins, the display of which to the covetous eyes of the Tibetans was always the means of hastening the transaction of business. In small handfuls, after each of which the Tibetans swore that they had not another atom to sell, I managed, with somewhat of a trial to my patience, to purchase some twenty pounds of food. The moment the money was handed over they had a quarrel among themselves about it, and almost came to blows, greed and avarice being the most marked characteristic of the Tibetans. No Tibetan of any rank is ashamed to beg in the most abject manner for the smallest silver coin, and when he sells and is paid, he always implores for another coin, to be thrown into the bargain, to obtain which, however small, a Tibetan of even a good position will stoop to almost any trick without thereby losing in the least the respect of his surroundings.

THE men of the party were extremely picturesque, with hair flowing down their shoulders and long pigtails ornamented with pieces of red cloth, circles of ivory, and silver coins. Nearly all had the stereotyped pattern coat, with ample sleeves hanging well over the hands, and pulled up at the waist to receive the paraphernalia of eating-bowls, snuff-box, etc., employed in daily life. Most of them were dressed in dark red, and all were armed with jewelled swords.

With flat, broad noses and slits of piercing eyes, high cheek-bones, and skin giving out abundant oily excretions, most of the men stood at a respectful distance, scrutinizing our faces and watching our movements apparently with much interest. I have hardly ever seen such cowardice and timidity as among these big, hulking fellows; to a European it hardly seems conceivable. The mere raising of one's eyes was sufficient to make a man dash away frightened, and, with the exception of the chief, who pretended to be unafraid, notwithstanding that even he was trembling with fear, they one and all showed ridiculous nervousness when I approached them to examine their clothes or the ornaments they wore round their necks, the most prominent of which were the charm-boxes that dangled on their chests. The larger of these

6

charm-boxes contained an image of Buddha, the others were mere brass or silver cases with nothing in them.

I was struck here, as well as in other camps, by the skill of the Tibetans in working leather, which they tan

TIBETAN YOUNG MAN

and prepare themselves, often giving to it a fine red or green color. As a rule, however, the natural tint is preserved, especially when the leather is used for belts, bullet and powder pouches, and flint-and-steel cases. The hair of the skins is removed by plucking and scraping, and preference is shown for skins of the yak, antelope, and kiang. The Tibetans are masters of the art of skinning, the hides being afterwards beaten, trodden upon, and manipulated to be rendered soft. There were simple ornamentations stamped upon some of the leather articles, but in most instances either metal or leather ornaments

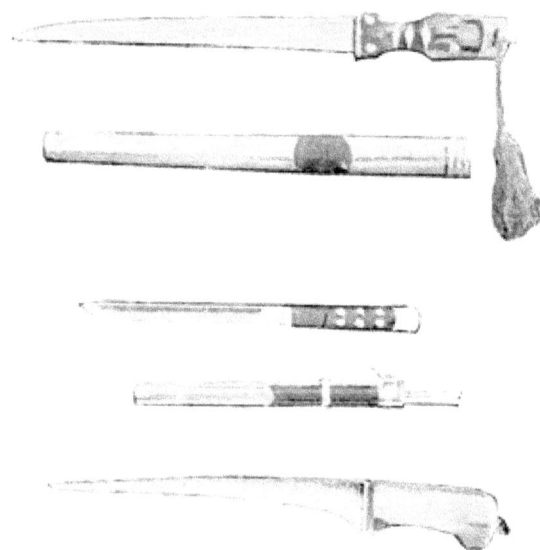

SWORDS

of various colors were fastened on the belts and pouches, iron clasps inlaid with silver, or silver ones, being the commonest.

These metals are found in the country, and the Tibetans smelt and cast the ore when sufficient fuel is obtainable for the purpose. Earthen crucibles are employed to liquefy the metals, and the castings are made in clay moulds. For the inlaid work, in which the Tibetans greatly excel, they use hammer and chisel. Inlaid ornamentation is frequently to be seen on the sheaths of

Tibetan swords, the leaf pattern, varied scrolls, and geometrical combinations being most commonly preferred. The process of hardening metals is still in its infancy, and Tibetan blades are of wrought-iron, and not of steel. They succeed, however, in bringing them to a wonderful

SADDLE

degree of sharpness, although they entirely lack the elasticity of steel blades. Grooves to let in air, and thus make wounds incurable, are generally ground in the sides of the daggers, but the blades of the common swords are perfectly smooth and made to cut on one side only. As can be seen from the illustrations, these weapons are hardly adapted to meet the requirements of severe fighting, as they do not allow a firm grip, nor have they any guard for the hand. The sheaths and handles of some of the more valuable swords are made of solid silver, inlaid with turquoises and coral beads, others of silver with gold ornamentations. At Lhassa and at Sigatz (Shigatze), silver filigree decorations are used on the best daggers; but nowhere else in Tibet is fine wire-making practised.

It must not be inferred from the above remarks that there are no steel swords in Tibet, for indeed many fine blades of excellent Chinese steel can be seen all over the country in the possession of the richer officials, such as the huge two-handed, double-edged swords of Chinese importation, used by Tibetan executioners.

The saddles, though possibly lacking comfort, are nevertheless skilfully made. The frame is made of solid wood (imported), and set in hammered iron (often inlaid with silver and gold, as in the saddle here reproduced), which, like a Mexican saddle, is very high in front and at the back. Lizard skin or colored leather is employed to decorate certain parts, and a pad covers the seat. A rug is, however, invariably placed over this pad for comfort, and the short iron stirrups compel one to sit with legs doubled up, a really not uncomfortable position when one gets used to it. Breast-piece, crupper, bridle, and bit are of leather ornamented with inlaid metal pieces. Double bags, for *tsamba*, butter, etc., are fastened behind the saddle, together with the inevitable peg and long rope, with which no Tibetan rider is unprovided, for the tethering of his pony at night.

Pack-saddles for yaks are made on the same principle, but are of much rougher construction, as can be judged from the illustrations* in which the two saddles I used on my journey are represented. The baggage is made fast by means of ropes to the two upper bars. To keep the saddle in position on the yak, and to prevent sores being inflicted, pads and blankets are laid upon the animal's back. Add to this protection the long coat possessed by the beast itself, and it will be clear why it very seldom sustains the slightest injury from these apparently cruel burdens.

CHAPTER LIII

WHEN night came on I did not consider it safe to en-
camp near the Tibetans. We moved away, driving our
yaks before us and dragging the newly purchased sheep.
We marched two and a half miles, and then halted in a
depression in the ground (16,050 feet), where we had a
little shelter from the wind, which blew with great force.
To our right lay a short range of fairly high mountains
running from north to south, and cut by a gorge, out of
which flowed a large stream. At that time of the evening we could not hope to cross it, but an attempt might
be made in the morning, when the cold of the night
would have checked the melting of the snows. Heavy
showers had fallen frequently during the day, and the
moment the sun went down there was a regular downpour. Our little *tente d'abri* had been pitched, but we
had to clear out of it a couple of hours later, the small
basin in which we had pitched it having been turned into
a regular pond. There was no alternative for us but to
come out into the open, for where the water did not flood
us the wind was so high and the ground so moist that it
was not possible to keep our tent up. The pegs would
not hold. The hours of the night seemed very long as
we sat tightly wrapped up in our waterproofs, with feet,
hands, and ears frozen, and the water dripping down upon

12

us. At dawn there were no signs of the storm abating.
We had not been able to light a fire in the evening, nor
could we light one now, and we were cold, hungry, and
miserable. The thermometer had been down to 36°. Towards
noon, the rain still pouring down in torrents and
there being no sign of its clearing, we loaded our yaks and
entered the gorge between the snow-covered mountains.
With difficulty we crossed the tributary we had so far
followed, and then proceeded along the right bank of the
main stream to 23° 30", then to 25°.

We were so exhausted and wet that when towards
evening we came to an enormous cliff, on the rocky face
of which a patient Lama sculptor had engraved in gigantic
letters the everlasting characters, "*Omne mani padme
hun,*" we halted. The gorge was very narrow here, and
we managed to find a dry spot under a big bowlder, but
as there was not sufficient room for all five, the two
Shokas went under the shelter of another rock a little
way off. This seemed natural enough, nor could I anticipate
any danger, taking care myself of the weapons and
the scientific instruments, while the Shokas had under
their own sheltering bowlder the bags containing nearly
all our provisions except tinned meats. The rain pelted
all night, the wind howled, and again we could not light
a fire. The thermometer did not fall below 38°, but the
cold, owing to our drenched condition, seemed intense.
In fact, we were so frozen that we did not venture to eat,
but, crouching ourselves in the small dry space at our disposal,
we eventually fell fast asleep without tasting food.
I slept soundly for the first time since I had been in
Tibet, and it was broad daylight when I woke up, to find
the man Nattoo from Kuti, and Bijesing the Johari, departed
from under their sheltering rock, together with the
loads intrusted to them. I discovered their tracks, half

washed away, in the direction from which we had come the previous night. The rascals had bolted, and there would have been comparatively little harm in that, if only they had not taken with them all the stock of provisions for my two Hindoo servants, and a quantity of good rope, straps, and other miscellaneous articles, which we were bound to miss at every turn, and which we had absolutely no means of replacing.

Of thirty picked servants who had started with me, twenty-eight had now abandoned me, and only two remained—faithful Chanden Sing and Mansing the leper!

The weather continued horrible, with no food for my men and no fuel! I proposed to the two to go back also and let me continue alone. I described to them the dangers of following me farther, and warned them fully, but they absolutely refused to leave me.

"Sahib, we are not Shokas," were their words. "If you die, we will die with you. We fear not death. We are sorry to see you suffer, sahib, but never mind us. We are only poor people, therefore it is of no consequence."

CHAPTER LIV

THIS last disaster should. I suppose, have deterred us
from further progress, but it somehow made me even
more determined to persist than I was before. It was no
light job to have to run afield one's self to capture the
yaks, which had wandered off in search of grass; and
having found them and driven them back to our primitive
camping-place, to tie upon their backs the pack-saddles,
and fasten on them the heavy tin-lined cases of scientific
instruments and photographic plates. This task was
only part of the day's routine, which included the writing
up of my diary, the registering of observations, sketching,
photographing, changing plates in cameras, occasionally
developing them, surveying, cleaning of rifles, revolver,
etc., etc. The effort of lifting up the heavy cases on to
the pack-saddles was, owing to our exhausted condition,
a severe tax on our strength, and the tantalizing restless-
ness of the yaks forced us to make several attempts before we actually succeeded in properly fastening the loads,
particularly as we had lost our best pieces of rope and
leather straps. Our sole remaining piece of rope seemed
hardly long enough to make the final knot to one of the
girths; anyhow, neither my bearer nor Mansing had sufficient strength to pull and make it join; so I made them
hold the yak by the horns to keep him steady while I
pulled my hardest. I succeeded with a great effort, and

15

was about to get up, when a terrific blow from the yak's horn struck me in the skull, an inch behind my right ear, and sent me rolling head over heels. I was stunned for several moments, and the back of my head was swollen and sore for many days, the mark of the blow being visible even now.

YAK WITH CASES OF SCIENTIFIC INSTRUMENTS

We proceeded along the right bank of the river on a course of 85° between reddish hills and distant high snowy mountains to the northwest and east-southeast of us, which we saw from time to time when the rain ceased and the sky cleared. The momentary lifting of the clouds would be followed by another downpour, and the marching became very unpleasant and difficult, as we sank deep in the mud. Towards evening we suddenly discovered some hundred and fifty soldiers riding full gallop in pursuit of us along the river valley. We pushed on, and having got out of their sight behind a hill, we deviated from our course and rapidly climbed up to the top of the hill range; my two men and the yaks concealed themselves on the other side. I remained lying flat on the top of the hill, spying with my telescope the movements of our

WITH ONLY TWO MEN I PROCEEDED TOWARDS LHASSA

pursuers. They rode unsuspectingly on, the tinkling of their horse-bells sounding pleasant to the ear at that deserted spot. They made a pretty picture, and, thinking probably that we had continued our way along the river, they rode past the spot where we had left the path, and, possibly owing to their haste to catch us up, did not notice our tracks up the hill-side.

Rain began to fall heavily again, and we remained encamped at 17,000 feet with all our loads ready for flight at any moment, the night being spent none too comfortably.

I sat up all night, rifle in hand, in case of a surprise, and I was indeed glad when day dawned. The rain had stopped, but we were now enveloped in a white mist which chilled us. I was very tired, and telling Chanden Sing to keep a sharp watch, tried to sleep for a while.

"*Hazur, hazur! jaldi apka banduk!*" (Sir, sir! quick, your rifle!) muttered my bearer, rousing me. "Do you hear the sound of bells?"

The tinkling was quite plain. As our pursuers were approaching, evidently in a strong body, there was no time to be lost. To successfully evade them appeared impossible. I decided to meet them rather than attempt flight. Chanden Sing and I were armed with our rifles, and Mansing with his Gourkha *kukri*, and thus we awaited their arrival. There came out of the mist a long procession of gray, phantom-like figures, each one leading a pony. The advance guard stopped from time to time to examine the ground; having discovered our footprints only partially washed away by the rain, they were following them up. Seeing us at last on the top of the hill, they halted. There was commotion among them, and they held an excited consultation: some of them unslung their matchlocks, others drew their swords, while we sat on a rock above and watched them with undivided attention.

CHAPTER LV

AFTER hesitating a little, four officers signalled to us that they wished to approach.

" You are a great king!" shouted one at the top of his voice, " and we want to lay these presents at your feet," and he pointed to some small bags which the other three men were carrying. "*Gelbo! Chakzal! Chakzal!*" (We salute you, king!)

I felt anything but regal after the wretched night we had spent, but I wished to treat the natives with due deference and politeness whenever it was possible.

I said that four men might approach, but the bulk of the party was to withdraw to a spot about two hundred yards away. This they immediately did, a matter of some surprise to me after the warlike attitude they had assumed at first. They laid their matchlocks down in the humblest fashion, and duly replaced their swords in their sheaths. The four officers approached, and when quite close to us, threw the bags on the ground and opened them to show us their contents. There was *tsamba*, flour, *chura* (a kind of cheese), *guram* (sweet paste), butter, and dried fruit. The officers were most profuse in their humble salutations. They had removed their caps and thrown them on the ground, and they kept their tongues sticking out of their mouths until I begged them to draw them in. They professed to be the subordinates of the

Tokchim Tarjum, who had despatched them to inquire after my health, and who wished me to look upon him as my best friend. Well aware of the difficulties we must encounter in travelling through such an inhospitable country, the Tarjum, they said, wished me to accept the gifts they now laid before me, and with these they handed me a *Kata*, or "the scarf of love and friendship," a long piece of thin silklike gauze, the ends of which had been cut into a fringe. In Tibet these *Katas* accompany every gift, and no caller ever goes about without one, which instantly on arrival he produces for presentation to his host. The high Lamas sell them to devotees, and one or more of these scarves is presented to those who leave a satisfactory oblation after visiting a Lamasery and temple. If a verbal message is sent to a friend, a *Kata* is sent with it, and among officials and Lamas small pieces of this silk gauze are enclosed even in letters. Not to give or send a *Kata* to an honored visitor is considered a breach of good manners, and is equivalent to a slight.

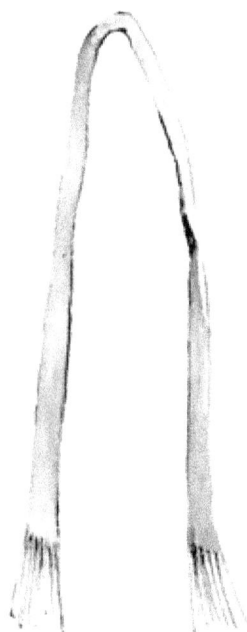

A KATA

I hastened to express my thanks for the Tarjum's kindness, and I handed the messengers a sum in silver of three times the value of the articles presented. The men seemed very pleasant and friendly, and we chatted for some time. Much to my annoyance, poor Mansing, bewildered at the sight of so much food, could no longer resist the pangs of hunger, and, caring little for the breach of etiquette and likely consequences, proceeded to fill his mouth with handfuls of flour, cheese, and butter. This led the Tibetans to suspect that we must be starving, and with their usual shrewdness they determined to take advantage of it.

"The Tarjum," said the oldest of the messengers, "wishes you to come back and be his guest, when he will feed you and your men, and you will then go back to your country."

"Thank you," I replied; "we do not want the Tarjum's food, nor do we wish to go back. I am greatly obliged for his kindness, but we will continue our journey."

"Then," angrily said a young and powerful Tibetan, "if you continue your journey we will take back our gifts."

"And your *Kata!*" I rejoined, sending first the large ball of butter flying into his chest, and after it the small bags of flour, *tsamba*, cheese, fruit, etc., a minute earlier prettily laid out before us.

This unexpected bombardment quite upset the Tibetans, who, with powdered coats, hair and faces, scampered away as best they could, while Chanden Sing, always as quick as lightning when it was a case of hitting, pounded away with the butt of his rifle at the roundest part of one ambassador's body, as in his clumsy clothes he attempted to get up and run.

Mansing, the philosopher of our party, interrupted in his feed but not put out, nor concerned in what was going on, picked up the fruit and cheese and pieces of butter scattered all over the place, mumbling that it was a shame to throw away good food in such a reckless fashion.

The soldiers, who had been watching attentively from a distance the different phases of the interview, considered it prudent to beat a hasty retreat, and, mounting their steeds with unmistakable dispatch, galloped pell-mell down the hill, and then along the valley of the river, until they were lost to sight in the mist, while the poor ambassadors, who had been unable to rejoin their ponies, followed as quickly as possible under the circumstances, considering the rarefied air and rough ground.

Their cries of distress, caused by fear alone, for we had done them no harm, served to strengthen the contempt in which my men by now held the Tibetan soldiers and their officers.

The scene really was comical, and I made as much capital as I could out of it, laughing with my companions and ridiculing to them the supposed valor of Tibetans.

When the Tibetans were out of sight, Chanden Sing and I pocketed our pride and helped Mansing to collect the dried dates, apricots, the pieces of *chura*, butter, and *guram*. Then having loaded our yaks we marched on.

CHAPTER LVI

RAIN IN TORRENTS—A SWAMPY PLAIN—THE SUN AT LAST—OUR YAKS
STOLEN AND RECOVERED

WE were not in luck. The weather continued squally
in the morning, and in the afternoon the rain was again
torrential. We went towards 78° over uninteresting and
monotonous gray country with a chain of snowy peaks
stretching from southwest to northeast. We waded
through a fairly deep and very cold river, and subsequently rose over a pass 17,450 feet. A number of Hunyas,
with flocks of several thousand sheep, came in sight, but
we avoided them. They did not see us.

At the point where we crossed it, the main stream
turns in a graceful bend to 140° (b. m.). We climbed over
hilly and barren country to an altitude of 17,550 feet,
where several small lakelets were to be found, and, having
marched in all fourteen and a half miles in a drenching
rain, we descended into a large valley. Here we had
great difficulty in finding a spot where to rest for the
night. The plain was simply a swamp, with several lakes
and ponds, and we sank everywhere in mud and water.
All our bedding and clothes were soaked to such an extent that it really made no difference where we halted; so
we pitched our little tent on the banks of a stream coming out of a valley to the north, from which, extending in
an easterly direction, rose a series of pyramidal mountains, covered with snow, and all of almost equal height
and base. To the south were high peaks with great

23

quantities of snow upon them. This valley was at an elevation of 17,450 feet, and the cold was intense.

At night the rain came down in bucketsful, and our *tente d'abri* gave us but little shelter. We were lying inside in water, and all the trenches in the world could not have kept it from streaming in. In fact, it is no exaggeration to say that the whole valley was a sheet of water from one to several inches deep. Of course, we suffered intensely from cold, the thermometer dropping to 26° at 8 P.M., when a southeast wind blew furiously; and the rain fell mixed with sleet for a time, and was followed by a heavy snow-storm. We lay crouched up on the top of our baggage, so as not to sleep on the frozen water, and when we woke in the morning our tent had half collapsed owing to the weight of snow upon it. During the day the temperature went up and rain fell afresh, so that when we resumed our marching we sank into a mixture of mud, snow and water several inches deep. We had to cross three rivers, and to skirt five lakes of varying sizes, following a course of 83° 45'.

Seven miles of this dreary marching saw us encamped (17,380 feet) by the foot of a conical hill 17,500 feet, where an almost identical repetition of the previous night's experience took place. The thermometer was down to 32°, but fortunately the wind subsided at eight in the evening. As luck would have it, the sun came out the following day, and we were able to spread out all our things to dry, during which process we had yet another novel experience.

Our two yaks had disappeared. I climbed up to the summit of the hill above camp, and with my telescope scoured the plain. The two animals were some distance off, being led away by ten or twelve men on horseback, who drove in front of them a flock of about five hundred

TORRENTIAL RAIN

sheep. By their clothing I recognized the strangers to be robbers. Naturally I started post haste to recover my property, leaving Chanden Sing and Mansing in charge of our camp. I caught them up as they marched slowly, though, when they perceived me, they hastened on, trying to get away. I shouted three times to them to stop, but they paid no heed to my words, so that I unslung my

HEAD OF BRIGAND

rifle, and would have shot at them had the threat alone not been sufficient to make them reflect. They halted, and when I got near enough I claimed my two yaks back. They refused to give them up. They said they were twelve men, and were not afraid of one. Dismounted from their ponies, they seemed ready to go for me.

As I saw them take out a flint and steel to light the fuses of their matchlocks, I thought I might as well have my innings first, and, before they could guess at my intention, I applied a violent blow with the muzzle of my rifle to the stomach of the man nearest to me. He collapsed, while I administered another blow to the right temple of another man who held his matchlock between his legs, and was on the point of striking his flint and steel to set the tinder on fire. He, too, staggered and fell clumsily.

BRIGANDS WITH SHEEP

" *Chakzal, chakzal! Chakzal wortzü!*" (We salute you, we salute you! Please listen!) exclaimed a third brigand, with an expression of dismay, and holding up his thumbs with his fist closed in sign of approval.

" *Chakzal,*" I replied, shoving a cartridge into the Mannlicher.

" *Middü, middü!*" (No, no!) they entreated, promptly laying down their weapons.

26

I purchased from these men about thirty pounds of *tsamba* and eight of butter. and got one of them to carry this to my camp, while I, without further trouble, recovered my yaks and drove them back to where Chanden Sing and Mansing were busy lighting a fire to make some tea.

II.—C

SADDLE-BAGS

Towards noon, when our things had got almost dry in the warm sun, the sky became overclouded, and it again began to rain heavily. I was rather doubtful as to whether I should go over a pass some miles off to 93 (b. m.), or should follow the course of the river and skirt the foot of the mountains. We saw a large number of Tibetans travelling in the opposite direction to ours, and they all seemed much terrified when we approached them. We obtained from them a few more pounds of food, but they refused to sell us any sheep, of which they had thousands. I decided to attempt the first-mentioned route, and, making our way first over a continuation of the flat plateau, then over undulating ground, we came to two lakelets at the foot of the pass in question. The ascent was comparatively gentle, over snow, and we followed the river descending from the top. About half-way up on looking back we saw eight soldiers galloping towards us. We waited for them, and as soon as they came up to us they went through the usual servile salutations, depositing their arms on the ground to show that they had no intention of fighting. A long friendly palaver followed, the Tibetans professing their friendship for us and their willingness to help us to get on in any way in their power. This was rather too good to be true, and I suspected treachery, all

28

the more so when they pressed and entreated us to go
back to their tents, where they wished us to remain as
their highly honored guests, and where we should have
all the luxuries that human mind can conceive showered
upon us.   On further specification, these were found to
consist of presents of *chura*, cheese, butter, yak milk, and
tsamba, and they said they would sell us ponies if we required them.   The description was too glowing ; so, taking all things into consideration, and allowing for the in-
accuracy of speech of my interlocutors, as well as of
Tibetans in general, I thanked them from the bottom
of my heart and answered that I preferred to continue
my way and bear my present sufferings.

They perceived that I was not easy to catch, and, if anything, they respected me the more for it.   In fact, they
could not disguise their amazement at my having got so
far with only two men.   When I had given my visitors
some little present, we parted at last in a very friendly
manner.

We climbed up to the pass (18,480 feet), and before us
on the other side found a large stretch of flat land, some
two thousand feet lower.   I could see a lake, which I
took to be the Gunkyo.   Nevertheless, to make certain
of it, I left my men and yaks in the pass and went to
reconnoitre from a peak 19,000 feet high, northeast of us.
There was much snow, and the ascent was difficult and
tedious.   When I got to the top another higher peak
barred the view in front of me, so descending first and
then ascending again, I climbed this second summit,
finally reaching an elevation of 20,000 feet, and obtaining a good bird's - eye view of the country all round.
There was a long snowy range to the north, and directly under it, what I imagined to be a stretch of water,
judging from the mist and clouds forming above it

and from the grass on the lower portion of the mountains.

A hill range stood in my way, just high enough to conceal the lake behind it. I rejoined my men and we continued our march down the other side of the pass, sinking in deep, soft snow. We pitched our tent at a spot about five hundred feet higher than the plain below us, in a

PHANTOM-LIKE VISITORS

gorge formed by the two mountain sides coming close together. Notwithstanding that I was now quite accustomed to great altitudes, the ascent to 20,000 feet had caused a certain exhaustion, and I should have been glad of a good night's rest.

Mansing and Chanden Sing, having eaten some food, slept soundly, but I felt very depressed. I had a peculiar sense of unrest and of some evil coming to us during the night.

We were all three under our little tent, when I began to fancy there was some one outside. I do not know why the thought entered my head, for I heard no noise, but all the same I felt I must see and satisfy my curiosity. I peeped out of the tent with my rifle in hand, and saw a number of black figures cautiously crawling towards us. In a moment I was outside on my bare feet, running towards them and shouting at the top of my voice: "*Pila tedan tedang!*" (Look out, look out!) which caused a stampede among our ghost-like visitors. There were, apparently, numbers of them hidden behind rocks, for when the panic seized them the number of runaways was double or even treble that of the phantoms I had at first seen approaching. At one moment there seemed to be black ghosts springing out from everywhere, only, more solid than ghosts, they made a dreadful noise with their heavy boots as they ran in confusion down the steep descent and through the gorge. They turned sharply round the hill at the bottom and disappeared.

When I crawled inside the tent again Chanden Sing and Mansing, wrapped head and all in their blankets, were still snoring!

NATURALLY I passed a sleepless night after that, fearing that the unwelcome visitors might return. We
speculated much as to how the Tibetans had found us,
and we could not help surmising that our friends of the
previous afternoon must have put them on our track. However, such was the inconceivable cowardice shown on
every occasion by the Tibetans, that we got to attach no
importance to these incidents, and not only did they not
inspire us with fear, but they even ceased to excite or dis-
turb us much.

We went on as usual, descending to the plain, and
when we got half-way across it, I scoured the hills all
round with my telescope to see if I could discern traces
of our pusillanimous foe.

"There they are," cried Chanden Sing, who had the
most wonderful eyesight of any man I have known, as he
pointed at the summit of a hill where, among the rocks,
several heads could be seen peeping. We went on without taking further notice of them, and then they came
out of their hiding-place, and we saw them descending
the hill in a long line, leading their ponies. On reaching
the plain they mounted their steeds and came full gallop
towards us. They were quite a picturesque sight in their
dark-red coats or brown and yellow skin robes and their
vari-colored caps. Some wore bright-red coats with gold

THE GUNSA(?) LAKE

braiding, and Chinese caps. These were officers. The soldiers' matchlocks, to the rests of which red and white flags were attached, gave a touch of color to the otherwise dreary scenery of barren hills and snow, and the tinkling of the horse-bells enlivened the monotony of these silent, inhospitable regions. They dismounted some three hundred yards from us, and one old man, throwing aside his matchlock and sword in a theatrical fashion, walked unsteadily towards us. We received him kindly, and he afforded us great amusement, for in his way he was a strange character.

"I am only a messenger," he hastened to state, "and therefore do not pour your anger upon me if I speak to you. I only convey the words of my officers, who do not dare to come for fear of being injured. News has been received at Lhassa, from whence we have come, that a *Plenki* (an Englishman) with many men is in Tibet, and can be found nowhere. We have been sent to capture him. Are you one of his advance guard?"

"No," I replied, dryly. "I suppose that you have taken several months to come from Lhassa."

"Oh no! Our ponies are good," he answered, "and we have come quickly."

"*Chik, ni, sum, shi, nga, do, diu, ghich, gu, chu, chuck chick, chuck ni,*" the Tibetan counted, up to twelve, frowning and keeping his head inclined towards the right as if to collect his thoughts, at the same time holding up his hand, with the thumb folded against the palm, and turning down a finger as he called each number. The thumbs are never used in counting. "*Lum chuck ni niman!*" (Twelve days!) said he, "have we been on the road, and we have orders not to return till we have captured the *Plenki*. And you," asked he, inquisitively, "how long have you taken to come from Ladak?"

He said that he could see by my face that I was a Kashmeree, I being probably so burned and dirty that it was hard to distinguish me from a native. The old man cross-examined me to find out whether I was a *pundit* sent by the Indian Government to survey the country, and asked me why I had discarded my native clothes for

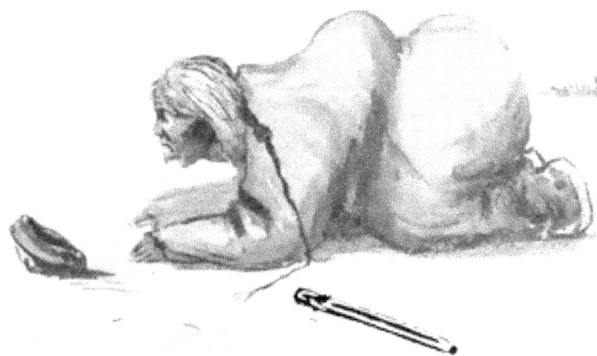

"I AM ONLY A MESSENGER"

Plenki (European) ones. He over and over again inquired whether I was not one of the *Plenki's* party.

"*Keran ga naddo ung?*" (Where are you going?) he queried.

"*Nhgarang ne koronn Lama jchlhuong*" (I am a pilgrim going to visit monasteries), I replied.

"*Keran mi japodn*" (You are a good man.)

He offered to show me the way to the Gunkyo Lake, and was so pressing that I accepted. However, when I saw the 200 soldiers mount and follow us, I remonstrated

54

with him, saying that if we were to be friends we did not need an army to escort us.

"If you are our friend, you can come alone, and we will not injure you," I gave him to understand; "but if you are our enemy we will fight you and your army here at once, and we will save you the trouble of coming on."

The Tibetan, confused and hesitating, went to confabulate with his men, and returned some time after with eight of them, while the bulk of his force galloped away in the opposite direction.

We went across the plain to 355° (b. m.), until we came to a hill range, which we crossed over a pass 17,450 feet high. Then, altering our course to 56° 30', we descended and ascended several hills, and at last found ourselves in the grassy sheltered valley of the large Gunkyo Lake, extending from southeast to northwest. With a temperature of 68° (Fahr.), the water in hypsometrical apparatus boiled at 183° 3½' at 8.30 in the evening. The lake was of extraordinary beauty, with the high snowy Gangri mountains rising almost sheer from its waters, and on the southern side lofty hills forming a background wild and picturesque, but barren and desolate beyond all words. At the other end of the lake, to the northwest, were lower mountains skirting the water.

We encamped at 16,455 feet, and the soldiers pitched their tent some fifty yards away.

DURING the evening the Tibetans came over to my
camp and made themselves useful. They helped us to get
fuel, and brewed tea for me in Tibetan fashion. They
seemed decent fellows, although sly if you like. They
professed to hate the Lamas, the rulers of the country, to
whom they took special pleasure in applying names hardly repeatable in these pages. According to them, the
Lamas had all the money that came into the country, and
no one but themselves was allowed to have any. They
were not particular as to the means used to obtain their
aim; they were cruel and unjust. Every man in Tibet,
they said, was a soldier in case of emergency, and every
one a servant of the Lamas. The soldiers of the standing army received a certain quantity of *tsamba*, bricks of
tea and butter, and that was all, no pay being given in
cash. Usually, however, they were given a pony to ride,
and when on travelling duty they had a right to obtain
relays of animals at post-stations and villages, where also
they were entitled to claim supplies of food, saddles, or
anything else they required, to last them as far as the
next encampment. The weapons (sword and matchlock) generally belonged to the men themselves, and always remained in the family; but occasionally, and especially in the larger towns, such as Lhassa and Sigatz,

FLYING PRAYERS ON THE MAIUM PASS

Lithographed by F. A. Brockhaus, Leipzig (Germany).

the Lamas provided them: gunpowder and bullets were invariably supplied by the authorities. The arms were manufactured mostly in Lhassa and Sigatz. Although the Tibetans boasted of great accuracy in shooting with their matchlocks, which had wooden rests to allow the marksman to take a steady aim, it was never my pleasure to see even the champion shots in the country hit the mark. It is true that for sporting purposes, and for economy's sake, the Tibetan soldier hardly ever used lead bullets or shot, but preferred to fill his barrel with pebbles, which were scarcely calculated to improve the bore of the weapon. Furthermore, gunpowder was so scarce that it was but very seldom they had a chance of practising.

At sunrise the view of Gunkyo was magnificent, with the snow-covered mountains tinted gold and red, and reflected in their minutest details in the still waters of the lake. We loaded our

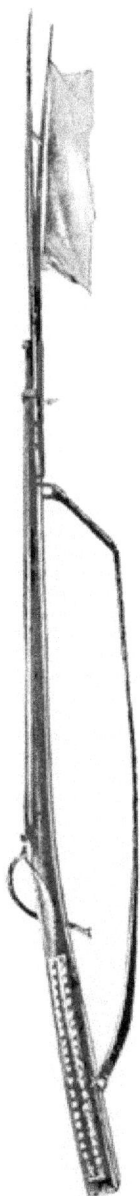

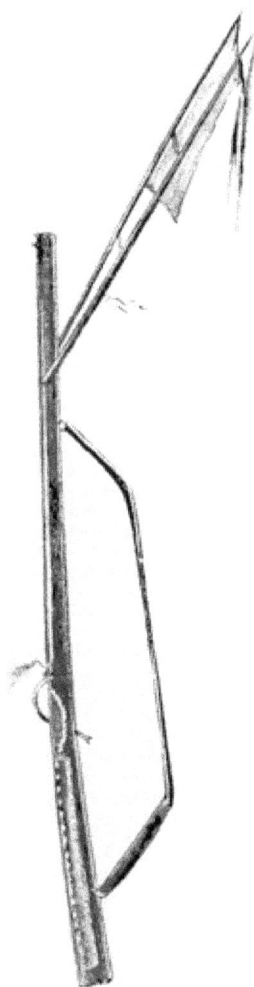

yaks, the Tibetans giving us a helping hand, and started towards the Maium Pass, following a general course of 109 up the river, which throws itself into the Gunkyo Lake.

The valley was very narrow, and ran in continuous zigzags; but although the altitude was great, there was abundance of grass, and the green was quite refreshing to the eyes, tired as we were of snow and reddish, barren mountains and desert-like stretches of land. We came to a basin where, on the opposite bank of the stream, was a large Tibetan camping-ground with a high wall of stones. Behind it I could see smoke rising, which made me suspect that there were people concealed there.

Our Tibetan friends asked what we were going to do, and begged me to stop there to talk and drink tea. I said I had had quite enough of both, and would proceed.

"If you go on we will kill you," said one of the soldiers, getting into a temper, and taking advantage of our politeness towards him and his mates.

"*Nga samgi ganta indah*" (If you please), I answered, with studied courtesy.

"If you go another step we will cut off your head, or you will have to cut off ours," cried two or three others, stretching their bare necks towards me.

"*Taptih middü*" (I have not got a small knife), I replied, quite seriously, and with assumed disappointment, twirling my hand in the air in Tibetan fashion.

The Tibetans did not know what to make of me, and when I moved towards the pass, on which hundreds of flying prayers flapped in the wind, after politely bidding them good-bye with tongue out, and waving both my hands, palms upwards, in front of my forehead in the most approved Tibetan style, they took off their caps and humbly saluted us by going down on their knees and putting their heads close to the ground.

We crossed the plain, and slowly wended our way up the pass. Near the top we came to a track, the highway from Ladak to Lhassa *via* Gartok, along the northern side of the Rakstal, Mansarowar, and Gunkyo Lakes. On the pass itself were planted several poles connected by means of ropes, from which flying prayers waved gayly in the breeze. *Obos*, or mounds of stones, had also been erected here. The slabs were usually white, and bore in many instances the inscription " *Omne mani padme hun.*" Yak skulls and horns, as well as those of goats and sheep, were laid by the side of these Obos, the same words being engraved on the bone, and stained red with the blood of the animal killed.

These sacrifices are offered by Tibetans when crossing a high pass, especially if there is a Lama close at hand to commemorate the event. The meat of the animal killed is eaten by the people present, and, if the party is a large one, dancing and singing follow the feast. As I have already remarked, these Obos are found all over the country ; they indicate the points marking the passes or summits of hills, and no Tibetan ever goes by one of them without depositing on it a white stone to appease the possible wrath of their God.

THE Maium Pass (17,500 feet), to which from where I started no Englishman had ever penetrated, is a great landmark in Hundes, for not only does one of the sources of the great Tsangpu, or Brahmaputra River, rise on its southeast slopes, but it also separates the immense provinces of Nari-Khorsum (extending west of the Maium Pass and comprising the mountainous and lacustrine region as far as Ladak) from the Yutzang, the central province of Tibet, stretching east of the pass along the valley of the Brahmaputra and having Lhassa for its capital. The word *Yu* in Tibetan means "middle," and it is applied to this province, as it occupies the centre of Tibet. To the north of the Maium lies the Doktol province.

I had taken a reconnoitring trip to another pass to the northeast of us, and had just returned to my men on the Maium Pass, when several of the Tibetan soldiers we had left behind rode up towards us. We waited for them, and their leader, pointing at the valley beyond the pass, cried: " That yonder is the Lhassa territory, and we forbid you to enter it."

I took no notice of his protest, and, driving before me the two yaks, I stepped into the most sacred of all the sacred provinces, " the ground of God."

ONE SOURCE OF THE BRAHMAPUTRA

We descended quickly on the eastern side of the pass, while the soldiers, aghast, remained watching us from above, themselves a most picturesque sight as they stood among the Obos against the sky-line, with the sunlight shining on their jewelled swords and the gay red flags of

SOURCE OF THE BRAHMAPUTRA

their matchlocks, while over their heads strings of flying prayers waved in the wind. Having watched us for a little while, they disappeared.

A little rivulet, hardly six inches wide, descended among stones in the centre of the valley we were following, and was soon swollen by other rivulets from melting snows on the mountains to either side. This was one source* of the great Brahmaputra, one of the largest rivers of the world. I must confess that I felt somewhat proud to be the first European who had ever reached these sources, and there was a certain childish delight in

* I passed the other source on the return journey.

standing over this sacred stream, which, of such immense width lower down, could here be spanned by a man standing with legs slightly apart. We drank of its waters at the spot where it had its birth, and then, following a marked track to 125° (b. m.), we continued our descent on a gentle incline along a grassy valley. The change in the climate between the west and southeast sides of the Maium Pass was extraordinary. On the western side we had nothing but violent storms of hail, rain, and snow, the dampness in the air rendering the atmosphere cold even during the day. The soil was unusually marshy, and very little fuel or grass could be found. The moment the pass was crossed we were in a mild, pleasant climate, with a lovely deep-blue sky over us and plenty of grass for the yaks, as well as low shrubs for our fires ; so that, after all our sufferings and privations, we felt that we had indeed entered the land of God. Notwithstanding that I expected great trouble sooner or later, I was not at all sorry I had disobeyed the soldiers' orders and had marched straight into the forbidden territory—it was a kind of wild satisfaction at doing that which is forbidden.

The Brahmaputra received three small snow-fed tributaries descending rapidly from the steep mountains on either side of us; and where the main stream turned sharply to 170°, a fourth and important tributary, carrying a very large volume of water, came down to it through a gorge from 20 (b. m.).

We encamped near the junction of these rivers, on the right bank of the main stream, at an altitude of 16,620 feet. From the Maium Pass a continuation of the Gangri chain of mountains runs first in a southeasterly direction, then due east, taking a line almost parallel to the higher southern range of the Himahlyas, and forming a vast plain intersected by the Brahmaputra. On the southern side of the river can be seen minor hill ranges between the river course and the big range with its majestic snowy peaks and beautiful glaciers. The northern range keeps an almost parallel line to the greater range southward; and, though no peaks of very considerable elevations are to be found along it, yet it is of geographical importance, as its southern slopes form the northern watershed of the holy river as far as Lhassa.

The valley enclosed between these two parallel ranges is the most thickly populated valley in Tibet. Grass is abundant, and fuel easily obtainable, and therefore thousands of yaks, sheep, and goats can be seen grazing near the many Tibetan camps along the Brahmaputra and its principal tributaries. The trade route taken by the caravans from Ladak to Lhassa follows this valley; and, as I came to Tibet to see and study the Tibetans, I thought that, although I might run greater risks, I could in no part of the country accomplish my object better than by going along this thickly populated track, which, moreover, had never before been trodden by a European.

WE slept very little, as we expected the soldiers to attack us during the night to try and stop our progress, but all was quiet and nothing happened; our yaks, however, managed to get loose, and we had some difficulty in recovering them in the morning, for they had swum across the stream, and had gone about a mile from camp on the other side.

The night had been very cold, the thermometer dropping as low as $32\frac{1}{2}$. We did not pitch our little tent, in case of emergencies, and we were tired and cold after the long march of the previous day. There was a southwesterly breeze blowing, and I found it hard to have to cross the river, chase the yaks and bring them back to camp. Then, exhausted as we were, we had in addition to go through the daily routine of loading them. We followed the right bank of the stream to bearings 170 (m.), then to 142 30' (b. m.), where it wound in and out between barren hills, subsequently flowing through a grassy valley three-quarters of a mile wide and a mile and a half long. It then went through a narrow passage to 17 30' (b. m.) and turned to 103 and farther to 142 through an undulating grassy valley two miles wide, in crossing which we were caught in a terrific thunderstorm, with hail and rain. This was indeed an annoying experience, for we were now before a very large tributary of the Brahmaputra, and the stream was so swollen, rapid, and deep that I was much puzzled as to how to take my men across: they could not swim, and the water was so cold that a dip in it would give any one a severe shock. However, there was no time to be lost, for the river was visibly rising, and, as the storm was getting worse, difficulties would only increase every moment. We took off every stitch of clothing and fastened our garments, with our rifles, etc., on the pack-saddles of the yaks, which we sent into the water. They are good swimmers, and though the current carried them over a hundred yards down stream, we saw them with satisfaction scramble out of the water on to the opposite bank. Notwithstanding the faith that Chanden Sing and Mansing had in my swimming, they really thought that their last hour had come when I took each by the hand and asked them to follow me into the stream. Hardly had we gone twelve yards when the inevitable took place. We were all three swept away, and Chanden Sing and Mansing in their panic clung tight to my arms and dragged me under water. Though I swam my hardest with my legs, we continually came to the surface and then sank again, owing to the dead weight of my helpless mates. But at last, after a desperate struggle, the current washed us on to the opposite side, where we found our feet, and were soon able to scramble out of the treacherous river. We were some two hundred yards down stream from the spot at which we had entered the river, and such was the quantity of muddy water we had swallowed that we all three became sick. This left us much exhausted, and, as the storm showed no signs of abating, we encamped (16,320 feet) there and then on the left bank of the stream. Though we sadly needed some warm food, there was, of course, no possibility of lighting a fire. A piece of chocolate was all I had that night, and my men preferred to eat nothing rather than break their caste by eating my food.

We were asleep under our little tent, the hour being about eleven, when there was a noise outside as of voices

A TIBETAN DOG.

and people stumbling against stones. I was out in a moment with my rifle, and shouted the usual "*Palado!*" (Go away!), in answer to which, though I could see nothing owing to the darkness, I heard several stones flung from slings whizzing past me. One of these hit the tent, and a dog barked furiously. I fired a shot in the air, which had the good effect of producing a hasty retreat of our enemies, whoever they were. The dog, however, would not go. He remained outside barking all night, and it was only in the morning, when I gave him some food and caressed him in Tibetan fashion, with the usual words of endearment, "*Chochu, Chochu,*" that our four-footed foe

SMALL MANI WALL

became friendly, rubbing himself against my legs as if he had known me all his life, and taking a particular fancy to Mansing, by whose side he lay down. From that day he never left our camp, and followed us everywhere, until harder times came upon us.

THE river was turning too much towards the south, so
I decided to abandon it and strike across country, especially as there were faint signs of a track leading over
a pass to 110 (b. m.) from camp. I followed this track,
and along it I distinguished marks of hundreds of ponies'
hoofs, now almost entirely washed away. This was evidently the way taken by the soldiers we had encountered
on the other side of the Maium Pass.

Having risen over the col 17,750 feet, we saw before
us an extensive valley with barren hills scattered over it.
To the south we observed a large plain some ten miles
wide, with snowy peaks rising on the farther side. In
front was a hill projecting into the plain, on which stood
a *mani* wall, and this latter discovery made me feel quite
confident that I was on the high-road to Lhassa. About
eight miles off to the north-northwest were high snowy
peaks, and as we went farther we found a lofty mountain
range, with still higher peaks, three miles behind it. We
had travelled half-way across the waterless plain, when
we noticed a number of soldiers' heads and matchlocks
popping in and out from behind a distant hill. After a
while they came out in numbers to observe our movements, then retired again behind the hill. We proceeded, but when we were still half a mile from them they

abandoned their hiding-place and galloped away before us, raising clouds of dust. From a hill 16,200 feet, over which the track crossed, we perceived a group of very high snowy peaks about eight miles distant. Between them and us stood a range of hills cut by a valley, along which flowed a river carrying a large volume of water. This we followed to 126° (b. m.), and, having found a suit-

AN EFFECT OF MIRAGE

able fording-place, we crossed over at a spot where the stream was twenty-five yards across, and the water reached up to our waists. We found here another *mani* wall with large inscriptions on stones, and, as the wind was very high and cutting, we made use of it to shelter ourselves. Within the angle comprised between bearings 240° and 120° (b. m.) we could observe a very high snowy mountain range in the distance (the great Himahlyan chain), and lower hill ranges even as near as three miles from camp.

The river we had just crossed flowed into the Brahmaputra, and we were now at an elevation of 15,700 feet. We saw plainly at sunset a number of black tents before us at bearings 120 ; we calculated them to be two miles distant. We counted about sixty, as well as hundreds of black yaks.

At sunrise the next morning, much to our surprise, they had all vanished; nor, on marching in the direction where we had seen them the previous night, were we able to find traces of them. It seemed as if it must have been mirage. Eventually, however, some fourteen miles away, across a grassy plain bounded to the northeast by the range extending from northwest to southeast, and with lofty snowy peaks at 72 some five miles off, we came upon a very large Tibetan encampment of over eighty black tents at an altitude of 15,650 feet. They were pitched on the banks of another tributary of the Brahmaputra, which, after describing a great curve in the plain, passed west of the encampment. Five miles off, in the arc of circle described from 310 to 70 (b. m.), stood the chain of mountains which I had observed all along; but here the elevations of its peaks became gradually lower and lower, so much so that the name of "hill range" would be more appropriate to it than that of "mountain chain." Behind it, however, towered loftier peaks again with their snowy caps.

CHAPTER LXIII

WE wanted food, and so made boldly for the encampment. Our approach caused a great commotion, and yaks and sheep were hastily driven away before us, while men and women rushed in and out of their tents, apparently in a state of much excitement. Eight or ten men reluctantly came forward and entreated us to go inside a large tent. They said they wished to speak to us, and offered us tea. I would not accept their invitation, distrusting them, but went on across the encampment, halting some three hundred yards beyond it. Chanden Sing and I proceeded afterwards on a round of calls at all the tents, trying to purchase food and also to show that, if we had declined to enter a particular tent, it was not on account of fear, but because we did not want to be caught in a trap. Our visit to the different *golingchos* or *gurr* (tents) was interesting enough. The tents themselves were very cleverly constructed, and admirably adapted to the country in which they were used; and the various articles of furniture inside attracted my curiosity. The tents, black in color, were woven of yaks' hair, the natural greasiness of which made them quite waterproof. They consisted of two separate pieces of this thick material, supported by two poles at each end, and there was an oblong aperture above in the upper part of the tent, through which the smoke could escape. The base of the larger tents was hexagonal in shape: the roof, generally at a height of six or seven feet above the ground, was kept very tightly stretched by means of long ropes passing over high poles and pegged to the ground. Wooden and iron pegs were used for this purpose, and many were required to keep the tent close to the ground all round, so as to protect its inmates from the cutting winds of the great plateau.

BLACK TENT

Long poles, as a rule numbering four, with white flying prayers, could be seen outside each tent, or one to each point of the compass, the east being taken for a starting-point. Around the interior of the larger tents there was a mud wall from two to three feet high, for the purpose of further protection against wind, rain, and snow. These walls were sometimes constructed of dried dung, which, as time went on, was used for fuel. There were two apertures, one at either end of the tent; that facing the wind being always kept closed by means of loops and wooden bolts.

The Tibetan is a born nomad, and shifts his dwelling with the seasons, or wherever he can find pasture for his yaks and sheep; but, though he has no fixed abode, he knows how to make himself comfortable, and he carries with him all that he requires. Thus, for instance, in the centre of his tent, he begins by making himself a *goling*, or fireplace of mud and stone, some three feet high and four or five long, by one and a half wide, with two, three, or more side ventilators and draught-holes. By this ingenious contrivance he manages to increase the combustion of the dried dung, the most trying fuel from which to get a flame. On the top of this stove a suitable place is made to fit the several *raksangs*, or large brass pots and bowls, in which the brick tea, having being duly pounded in a stone or wooden mortar, is boiled and stirred with a long brass spoon. A portable iron stand is generally to be seen somewhere in the tent, upon which the hot vessels are placed as they are removed from the fire. Close to these is the *toxzum* or *dongbo*, a cylindrical wooden churn, with a lid through which a piston passes. This is used for mixing the tea with butter and salt, in the way I have described as also adopted by the Jopgas.

A DONGBO, OR TEA CHURN

The wooden cups or bowls used by the Tibetans are called *puku*, *fruh*, or *cariel*, and in them *tsamba* is also eaten after tea has been poured on it, and the mixture worked into a paste by means of more or less dirty fingers. Often extra lumps of butter are mixed with this paste, and even bits of *chura* (cheese). The richer people (officials) indulge in flour and rice, which they import from

India and China, and in *kassur*, or dried fruit (namely, dates and apricots) of inferior quality. The rice is boiled into a kind of soup called the *tukpa*, a great luxury only indulged in on grand occasions, when such other cherished delicacies as *gimakara* (sugar) and *shelkara* (lump white sugar) are also eaten. The Tibetans are very fond of meat, though few can afford such an extravagance. Wild game, yak, and sheep are considered excellent food, and the meat and bone cut in pieces are boiled in a cal-

TRAMGO   SMALL TRAMBA BAG, CARRIED ON THE PERSON BY TIBETANS

dron with lavish quantities of salt and pepper. The several people in a tent dip their hands into the pot, and, having picked up suitable pieces, tug at them with their teeth and fingers, grinding even the bone, meat eaten without bone being supposed to be difficult to digest.

The Tibetan tents are usually furnished with a few *tildih* (rough sitting-mats) round the fireplace, and near the entrance of the tent stands a *dahlo*, or basket, in which the dung is stored as collected. These *dahlos*, used in couples, are very convenient for tying to pack-saddles, for which purpose they are specially designed. Along the walls of the tent are the *tsamgo* or bags of *tsamba*, and the *dongmo*, or butter - pots, and among masses of sheepskins and blankets be seen the little wooden chests in which the store of butter is kept under lock and key.

The first thing that strikes the eye on entering a Tibetan tent is the *choksah*, or table, upon which are lights and brass bowls containing offerings to the *Chogan*, the gilt god to whom the occupiers of the *gurr* (tent) address their morning and evening prayers. Prayer-wheels and strings of beads are plentiful, and lashed upright to the poles are the long matchlocks belonging to the men, their tall props projecting well out of the aperture in the roof of the tent. Spears are kept in a similar manner, but the swords and smaller knives are carried about the person all day, and laid on the ground by the side of their owners at night.

CHAPTER LXIV

THE inhabitants of this encampment were polite and
talkative. Notwithstanding their refusal to sell us food
on the plea that they had none even for themselves, their
friendliness was so much beyond my expectation that I
at first feared treachery. However, treachery or not, I
thought that while I was there I had better see and learn
as much as I could. Women and men formed a ring
round us, and the fair sex seemed less shy than the
stronger in answering questions. I was particularly
struck, not only in this encampment, but in all the others,
by the small number of women to be seen in Tibet.
This is not because they are kept in seclusion; on the
contrary, the ladies of the Forbidden Land seem to have
it all their own way. They are actually in an enormous
minority, the proportion being, at a rough guess, backed
by the wise words of a friendly Lama, from fifteen to
twenty males to each female in the population; nevertheless, the fair sex in Hundes manages to rule the male
majority, playing thereby constantly into the hands of the
Lamas.

The Tibetan female, whether she be a lady, a shep-
herdess, or a brigandess, cannot be said to be prepossess-
ing. In fact, it was not my luck to see a single good-
looking woman in the country, although I naturally saw
women who were less ugly than others. Anyhow, with

56

TIBETAN WOMEN AND CHILDREN

the accumulated filth that from birth is undisturbed by soap, scrubbing, or bathing; with nose, cheeks, and fore-head smeared with black ointment to prevent the skin cracking in the wind; and with the unpleasant odor that emanates from never-changed clothes, the Tibetan woman

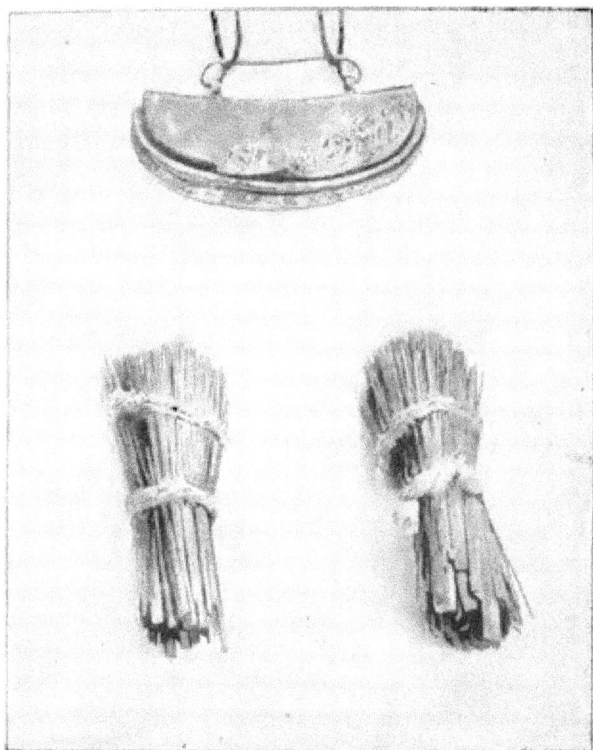

TIBETAN HAIR-BRUSHES AND FLINT-AND-STEEL POUCH

is, at her best, repulsive to European taste. After one has overcome one's first disgust, she yet has, at a distance, a certain charm of her own. She walks well, for she is accustomed to carry heavy weights on her head; and her skull would be well-set on her shoulders were it not that the neck is usually too short and thick to be graceful.

57

Her body and limbs possess great muscular strength and are well developed, but generally lack stability, and her breasts are flabby and pendent—facts due, no doubt, to sexual abuse. She is generally of heavy frame, and rather inclined to stoutness. Her hands and feet show power and rude strength, but no dexterity or suppleness is noticeable in her fingers, and she has therefore no ability for very fine or delicate work.

The Tibetan woman is, nevertheless, far superior to the Tibetan man. She possesses a better heart, more pluck, and a finer character than he does. Time after time, when the males, timid beyond all conception, ran away at our approach, the women remained in charge of the tents, and, although by no means cool or collected, they very rarely failed to meet us without some show of dignity.

On the present occasion, when all were friendly, the women seemed much less shy than the men, and conversed freely and incessantly. They even prevailed upon their masters to sell us a little *tsamba* and butter.

Tibetan women wear trousers and boots like the men, and over them they have a long gown, either yellow or blue, reaching down to their feet. Their head-dress is curious, the hair being carefully parted in the middle, and plastered with melted butter over the scalp as far down as the ears; then it is plaited all round in innumerable little tresses, to which is fastened the *Tchukti*, three strips of heavy red-and-blue cloth joined together by iron bands ornamented with coral and malachite beads and silver coins and bells, and reaching from the shoulders down to the heels.

They seemed very proud of this ornamentation, and displayed much coquetry in attracting our notice to it. Wealthier women in Tibet have quite a small fortune

A LADY FROM LHASSA

THE TCHUKTI

hanging down their backs, for all the money or valuables earned or saved are sewn on to the *Tchukti*. To the lower end of the *Tchukti* one, two, or three rows of small brass or silver bells are attached, and therefore the approach of the Tibetan dames is announced by the tinkling of their bells, a quaint custom, the origin of which they could not explain to me, beyond saying that it was pretty and that they liked it.

The illustration that I give here of a travelling Tibetan lady from Lhassa was taken at Tucker. She wore her hair, of abnormal length and beauty, in one huge tress, and round her head, like an aureole, was a circular wooden ornament, on the outer part of which were fastened beads of coral, glass, and malachite. The arrangement was so heavy that, though it fitted the head well, it had to be supported by means of strings tied to the hair and others passed over the head. By the side of her head, and hanging by the ears and hair, were a pair of huge silver ear-rings inlaid with malachite, and round her neck three long strings of beads with silver brooches.

Considerable modifications necessarily occurred in these garments and ornaments, according to the locality and the wearer's condition in life, but the general lines of their clothing were practically everywhere the same. Often a loose silver chain belt was worn considerably below the waist, and rings and bracelets were common everywhere.

MONEY-BAGS

CHAPTER LXV

POLYANDRY—MARRIAGE CEREMONIES—JEALOUSY—DIVORCE—IDENTIFI-
CATION OF CHILDREN—COURTSHIP—ILLEGITIMACY—ADULTERY

THAT the Tibetans legally recognize polyandry and polygamy is well known. Very little, however, has hitherto transpired as to the actual form of these marital customs, so that the details which follow, startling as they may seem when regarded from a Western stand-point, will be found not without interest.

First of all, I may say that there is not such a thing known in Tibet as a standard of morality among unmarried women of the middle classes; and, therefore, from a Tibetan point of view, it is not easy to find an immoral woman. Notwithstanding this apparently irregular state of affairs, the women's behavior is better than might be expected. Like the Shoka girls, they possess a wonderful frankness and simplicity of manner, with a certain reserve which has its allurements; for the Tibetan swain, often a young man, being attracted by the charms of a damsel, finds that his flirtation with her has become an accepted engagement almost before it has begun, and is compelled, in accordance with custom, to go, accompanied by his father and mother, to the tent of the lady of his heart. There he is received by her relations, who have been previously notified of the intended call, and are found seated on rugs and mats awaiting the arrival of their guests.

After the usual courtesies and salutations, the young

man's father asks, on behalf of his son, for the young
lady's hand; and, if the answer is favorable, the suitor
places a square lump of yak *murr* (butter) on his be-

WOMAN WHOSE FACE IS SMEARED WITH BLACK OINTMENT

trothed's forehead. She does the same for him, and the
marriage ceremony is then considered over, the buttered
couple being man and wife.

If there is a temple close by, *Katas*, food, and money
are laid before the images of god and saints, and the
parties walk round the inside of the temple. Should there

be no temple at hand, the husband and wife make the circuit of the nearest hill, or, in default of anything else, the tent itself, always moving from left to right. This ceremony is repeated with prayers and sacrifices every day for a fortnight, during which time libations of wine and general feasting continue, and at the expiration of which the husband conveys his better half to his tent.

The law of Tibet, though hardly ever obeyed, has strict clauses regulating the conduct of married men in their marital relations. So long as the sun is above the horizon, no intercourse is permitted; and certain periods and seasons of the year, such as the height of summer and the depth of winter, are also proscribed.

A Tibetan girl on marrying does not enter into a nuptial tie with an individual but with all his family, in the following somewhat complicated manner. If an eldest son marries an eldest sister, all the sisters of the bride become his wives. Should he, however, begin by marrying the second sister, then only the sisters from the second down will be his property. If the third, all from the third, and so on. At the same time, when the bridegroom has brothers, they are all regarded as their brother's wife's husbands, and they one and all cohabit with her, as well as with her sisters if she has any.

The system is not simple, and certainly not very edifying, and were it not for the odd *savoir faire* of the Tibetan woman, it would lead to endless jealousies and unpleasantness: owing, however, largely, no doubt, to the absolute lack of honor or decency in Tibetan males and females, the arrangement seems to work as satisfactorily as any other kind of marriage.

I asked what would happen in the case of a man marrying a second sister, and so acquiring marital rights over all her younger sisters, if another man came and married her eldest sister. Would all the brides of the first man become the brides of the second? No, they would not; and the second man would have to be satisfied with only one wife. However, if the second sister were left a widow, and her husband had no brothers, then she would

TIBETAN WOMAN

become the property of her eldest sister's husband, and with her all the other sisters.

It must not be inferred from these strange matrimonial laws that jealousy is non-existent in Tibet among both men and women; trouble does occasionally arise in Tibetan house or tent holds As, however, the Tibetan woman is clever, she generally contrives to arrange things in a manner conducive to peace. When her husband has several brothers, she despatches them on different errands in every direction, to look after yaks or sheep, or to trade.

Only one remaining, he is for the time being her husband; then when another returns he has to leave his place and becomes a bachelor, and so on, till all the brothers have, during the year, had an equal period of marital life with their single wife.

Divorce is difficult in Tibet and involves endless complications. I inquired of a Tibetan lady what would she do in case her husband refused to live with her any longer.

" 'Why did you marry me?' I would say to him," she exclaimed. " 'You found me good, beautiful, wise, clever, affectionate. Now prove that I am not all this!' "

This modest speech, she thought, would be quite sufficient to bring any husband back to reason, but all the same a number of Tibetans find it convenient occasionally to desert their wives, eloping to some distant province or over the boundary. This procedure is particularly hard on the man's brothers, as they all remain the sole property of the abandoned bride. On the same principle, when a husband dies, the wife is inherited by his brothers.

A very painful case came before the court of the Jong Pen at Taklakot. The husband of a Tibetan lady had died, and she, being enamored of a handsome youth some twenty years younger than herself, married him. Her husband's brother, however, came all the way from Lhassa after her and claimed her as his wife, though he had already a better half and a large family. She would not hear of leaving the husband of her choice, and after endless scenes between them the case was heard by the Jong Pen of Taklakot. The Tibetan law was against her, as, according to it, she decidedly belonged to her brother-in-law; but money is stronger than the law in the land of the Lamas.

" For the peace of all, you can arrange things this way,"

was the advice of the Jong Pen. "You can divide your property, money and goods, into three equal parts: one to go to the Lamas, one to your husband's brother, and one to be retained by yourself."

The woman consented; but, much to her disgust, when two parts had been paid out and she was hoping for peace, a question was raised by the Jong Pen as to why she should even retain one-third of the fortune if she no longer were part of the deceased man's family? Thus orders were instantly given that she should be deprived of everything she possessed.

However, the woman was shrewd enough to deceive the Jong Pen's officers, for one night, having bundled up her tent and her goods and chattels, she quietly stepped over the boundary and placed herself under British protection.

The mode of knowing and identifying children in Tibet is peculiar. It is not by the child's likeness to his parent, nor by other reasonable methods, that the offspring is set down as belonging to one man more than to another, but this is the mode adopted. Supposing that one married man had two brothers and several children, the first child belongs to him, the second to his first brother, and the third to his second brother, while the fourth would be again the first man's child.

The rules of courtship are not very strict in Tibet, yet intercourse with girls is looked upon as illegal, and in certain cases not only are the parties, if discovered, made to suffer shame, but certain fines are inflicted on the man, the most severe of all being that he must present the young lady with a dress and ornaments. In the case of "gentle-folks" the question is generally solved to the satisfaction of everybody by the man marrying the woman, and by his gracefully presenting "veils of friendship" to all her relations and friends, together with articles of food; but if by mischance she should be placed in an awkward position before the eyes of the world, and the man will not hear of a matrimonial union, then efforts

THE LADY IN QUESTION

are made to prevent the birth of the child alive. If these are not successful, the mother must be maintained until after the child's birth. In such cases the illegitimate child remains the man's, and suffers forever the usual indignities of illegitimacy.

Sixteen in the case of women, and eighteen or nineteen in that of men, is regarded as the marriageable age. Motherhood continues until a fairly advanced age, and I have seen a woman of forty with a baby only a few months old. But, as a rule, Tibetan women lose their freshness while still quite young; and no doubt their custom of polyandry not only contributes to destroy their looks but also is the chief cause that limits the population of Tibet.

The Lamas are supposed to live in celibacy, but they do not always keep to their oath, tempted, no doubt, by the fact that they themselves invariably go unpunished. If, on the other hand, the culprit be a layman, he has to pay compensation according to his means to the husband, the amount being fixed by the parties concerned and their friends, or by the law if applied for.

In ordinary cases of marital trespass, presents of clothing, *tsamba, chura, guram, kassur* (dried fruit) and wine, accompanied by the never-lacking *Kata*, are sufficient to allay the injured husband's anger and to fully compensate him for any shame suffered.

The only serious punishment inflicted is, however, in the case of the wife of a high official eloping with a man of low rank. Then the woman is subjected to flogging as a penalty for her infidelity, her husband is disgraced, and her lover, after being subjected to a painful surgical operation, is, if he survives, expelled from the town or encampment.

High officials, and a few wealthy people who are not satisfied with one wife, are allowed by the law of the land to keep as many concubines as their means allow them.

CHAPTER LXVI

TIBETAN FUNERALS — DISPOSAL OF THEIR DEAD — BY CREMATION—BY
WATER—CANNIBALISM—STRANGE BELIEFS — REVOLTING BARBARITY
—DRINKING HUMAN BLOOD—THE SAINTS OF TIBET

TIBETAN funerals are interesting, but they so closely
resemble those of the Shokas, which I have described at
length, that any detailed account of them would be a
mere repetition of what I have already written.

For the disposal of the dead body itself, however, the
Tibetans have curious customs of their own. The most
uncommon method, owing to the great scarcity of fuel, is
that of cremation, which is only employed in the case of
wealthy people or Lamas, and is effected in exactly the
same fashion as among the Shokas. Another and more
usual plan is to double up the body, sew it into skins,
and let it be carried away by the current of a stream.
But the commonest method of all is the revolting ceremony which I now proceed to describe.

The body of the deceased is borne to the top of a hill,
where the Lamas pronounce certain incantations and
prayers. Then the crowd, after walking seven times
round the body, retire to a certain distance, to allow
ravens and dogs to tear the corpse to pieces. It is considered lucky for the departed and his family when birds
alone devour the greater portion of the body; dogs and
wild animals come, say the Lamas, when the deceased
has sinned during his life. Anyhow, the almost com-
plete destruction of the corpse is anxiously watched, and,

at an opportune moment, the Lamas and crowd, turning their praying-wheels, and muttering the everlasting "*Omne mani padme hun*," return to the body, round which seven more circuits are made, moving from left to right.* Then the relatives squat round. The Lamas

A YOUNG LAMAS

sit near the body, and with their daggers cut to pieces what remains of the flesh. The higher Lama eats the first morsel, then, muttering prayers, the other Lamas partake of it, after which all the relations and friends throw themselves on the now almost denuded skeleton, scraping off pieces of flesh, which they devour greedily; and this repast of human flesh continues till the bones are dry and clean!

The idea of this ghastly ceremony is that the spirit of

In the case of a sect called Bombos, the circuits are made in the reverse fashion, as also are their prayer-wheels turned from right to left.

TIBETAN CHILDREN

the departed, of whom you have swallowed a piece, will forever keep on friendly terms with you. When birds and dogs do not shrink from feeding, it is a sign that the body is healthy, and fit for themselves.

Revolting beyond words is the further fact that, when a man has died of some pestilential disease, and, owing to the odor, the birds will not peck at the body, nor will the famished dogs go near it, then a large number of Lamas, having made the usual exorcisms, sit down by it, and do not get up again until they have devoured the whole of the rotten human flesh! The relatives and friends are wiser and less brutal. They rightly believe that, if voracious animals will not partake of the meal proffered them, it is because the body is that of a sinner against whom God is angry. And who better than the Lamas could make peace between God and him? So let the Lamas eat it all.

A RED LAMA

In the case of not finding sufficient Lamas to perform these rites, the body is either disposed of by throwing it into the water, or else, the relations having first partaken of a morsel of the flesh, it is bound to a rock to let animals or time do the rest.

The Lamas are said to have a great craving for human blood, which, they say, gives them strength, genius, and vigor. When sucking wounds that are not poisoned, they drink the blood, and also on certain occasions wounds are inflicted for the sake of sucking the blood. At other

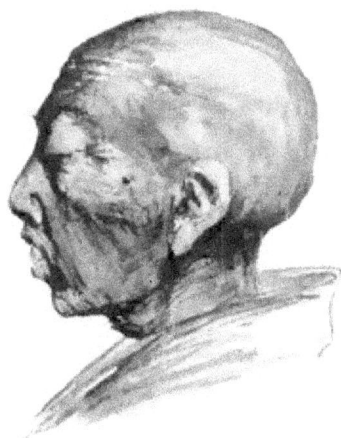

times the cups cut from human skulls, found in all monasteries, are filled with blood, and the Lamas in turn satisfy their thirst out of them.

CUP MADE OF HUMAN SKULL

But enough of this. It is sickening to set it down, though my book would be incomplete if I had made no mention of the cannibalism of the Lamas.

When a saintly Lama dies, or some old man much re-

CHOKDEN, OR TOMB OF A SAINT

spected by the community, either parts of the flesh, or, if cremation has been applied, some of his ashes, are preserved and placed in a *Chokden* erected for the purpose; and, judging by the number of these structures one finds all over Tibet, one feels inclined to think that half the population of the country must have been saints, or else that the standard of saintliness in the sacred land of the Lamas is not prohibitively high.

CHAPTER LXVII

COMING out of our tent in the morning, we noticed an unusual commotion among the Tibetans. A number of mounted men with matchlocks had arrived, and others similarly armed immediately went to join them from the tents. They seemed excited, and I kept my eye upon them while I was cooking my food. There were some two hundred in all, picturesquely garbed. They seemed to be good horsemen, and looked well as they rode in a line towards us. A little way off they stopped and dismounted, and the leaders came forward, one stalwart fellow in a fine sheepskin coat marching ahead of the rest. His attitude was very arrogant, and, dispensing with the usual salutations, he approached quite close, shaking his fist at me.

"*Kiu mahla lokhna nga rah luck tiba tangan*" (I will give you a goat or a sheep if you will go back), he said.

"*Kiu douna nga di tangon!*" (And I give you this to make you go back!) was my quick answer, while I unexpectedly administered him one straight from the shoulder that sent him flat on his back and sprawling on the ground.

The Tibetan army, which, with its usual prudence, was watching events from a respectful distance, beat a hasty retreat. The officer, though unhurt, scrambled away, screaming. The Tibetans had so far behaved with such

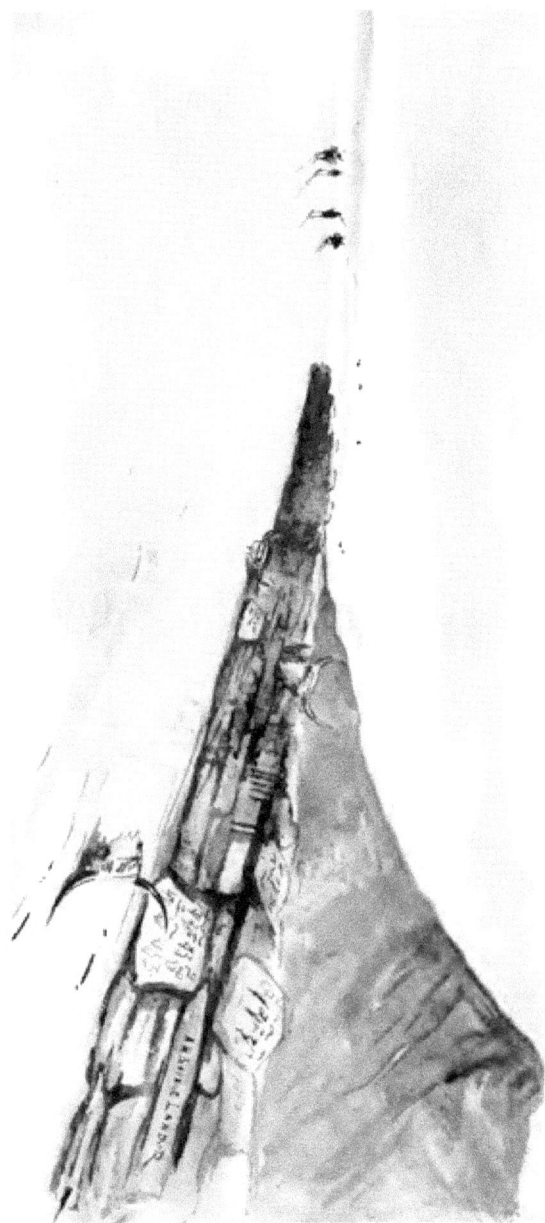

contemptible cowardice that we could hardly congratulate ourselves on such easy successes. We began to feel that really we had no enemy at all before us, and very likely we became even careless. Anyhow, we ate our food and gave this affair but little thought.

Our progress was now comparatively easy, along a broad grassy plain, and we proceeded without further dis-

"AND I GIVE YOU THIS TO MAKE YOU GO BACK"

turbance in a southeasterly direction, observing a high snowy peak at 20° (b. m.), and a low pass in the mountain range to our northeast at 55° (b. m.). A very high range stood ahead of us in the far distance, with low hills between. In going round one of these lonely hills we found at the foot of it another and more important *mani* wall of some length, with numberless inscriptions of all ages and sizes on stones, pieces of bone, skulls, and horns. Farther on, to the south, there were three smaller hillocks and two larger ones. The soldiers we had routed at the encampment had proceeded in the direction we were now following, and we were, in fact, treading all along on the footprints of their ponies.

We had to cross a river and a number of rivulets, and so troublesome was it each time to take off one's shoes and clothes to wade through, that we bundled up our clothes on the yaks, and travelled along for the rest of the afternoon barefooted and with nothing on but a *doti* (loin-cloth), in the style adopted by fakirs.

In an arc of a circle from 120° to 180° (b. m.) we noticed very low hills, and from 160° to 220°, some thirty or forty miles off, could be seen much more clearly now the high range we had observed before. The sun was extremely hot, the ground marshy, the air being thick with huge and very troublesome mosquitoes. We were quickly covered from head to foot with bites, and the irritation caused by them was intense. Halting on the right bank of a large stream at 15,600 feet, we named this spot Mosquito Camp. At sunset the number of mosquitoes around us was such as to drive us nearly mad, but fortunately the moment the sun disappeared the thermometer fell to 33°, and we had a peaceful night.

In the evening we saw a number of horsemen riding full speed on a course about one mile south of ours, but converging to the same direction. No doubt they were sent to keep the authorities ahead well informed of our movements.

THE next was for us a great washing-day. The water
of the stream was so pleasant and clear that we could not
resist the temptation of having a regular cleaning up,
washing first our clothing and spreading it to dry in the
sun, and then cleansing our faces and bodies thoroughly
with soap, a luxury unknown to us for ever so long.

While I was drying myself in the sun—owing to the
want of towels—I registered at 211° (b. m.) a very high
snowy peak, and a lower one at 213' 30' forming part of
the chain before us. There were mountains on every side
of the plain we were traversing; and another very ele-
vated peak, of which I had taken bearings on a previous
occasion, was at 20° (b. m.). A break occurred in the hill
range to our northeast, showing a narrow valley, beyond
which were high snowy mountains on either side. We
made a very long march along the grassy plain, going to
147° (b. m.), and encamped on the bank of the Brahmaputra, here already a wide, deep, and very rapid stream.
We had passed hundreds of *kiang* and antelopes, and
shortly before sunset I took a walk to the hills to try and
bring some fresh meat to camp. I stalked a herd of antelopes, and having gone some five miles from camp, I
was benighted, and on my return had the greatest difficulty in finding my men in the darkness. They had been

unable to light a fire, and as they had both gone fast asleep, I received no answer to my calls. We had selected a sheltered depression in the ground for our camp, and there being hundreds of similar spots everywhere round it, and no landmarks to go by, it was by no means easy to identify the exact place.

Fortunately, at last, after I had shouted for some considerable time, Chanden Sing heard me, and, by the sound of his voice, I found my way back. In the morning we noticed a large encampment about a mile off, on the opposite bank of the Brahmaputra, where we might have obtained provisions, but the stream was too rapid for us to cross; moreover, we saw black tents in every direction on our side of the water, and therefore there was no reason to go to the extra trouble and danger of crossing the stream.

Much to our delight, we succeeded in purchasing a goat from some passing Tibetans, who drove before them a flock of several thousand heads, and, as we could not find sufficient dry fuel to make a fire, we intrusted Mansing with the safe conduct of the animal to our next camp, where we proposed to feast on it.

The Brahmaputra had here several ramifications, mostly ending in lakelets, and rendering the plain a regular swamp. The larger branch was very wide and deep, and we preferred following it to crossing it, notwithstanding that we had to deviate somewhat from the course which I would have otherwise followed. We thus made a considerable détour, but as it was, even for several miles we sank in mud up to our knees, or waded through water, out of which rose small patches of earth with tufts of grass that collapsed on our attempting to stand upon them.

The whole of the northern part of the plain was extremely marshy. Our yaks gave us no end of trouble,

78

for when they sank unexpectedly in soft mud-holes, they became restless and alarmed, and in their struggles to save themselves, once or twice shook off their pack-saddles and loads, which we had not been able to fasten properly for want of ropes. Chanden Sing and I, how-

OUR YAKS SINKING IN MUD

ever, managed to keep up with them, and at last, on nearing the hills, the ground showed greater undulations and was rather drier. We saw columns of smoke rising from near the foot of the range to the north of us. We went on another couple of miles, exhausted and dirty, our clothes, which we had spent so much soap and time in washing, filthy with splashes of mud.

"Where is Mansing? and the *rabbu*?"* I asked of my bearer.

* The Tibetans have three distinct kinds of goats—the *rabbu*, or large woolly animal, such as the one I had purchased; the *rattou*, or small goat;

" He remained behind at the beginning of the swamp. He was too exhausted to drag along the goat you purchased."

I was much concerned, on scouting the country all round from a hillock with my telescope, to see no signs of the poor fellow, and I was angry with myself for not

KIANG

noticing his disappearance before. As there were many Tibetans about the spot where he had remained, I feared foul play on their part, and that he might have been overpowered. Again I imagined that, weak as he was, he might have been sucked down in one of the deeper mudholes, without a chance of saving himself. I left Chanden Sing to look after the yaks and turned back in search of him. As I hurried back mile after mile, struggling again

and the *chibu*, a dwarf goat whose flesh is delicious eating. The *rabbu* and *ratton* are the two kinds generally used for carrying loads, and they have sufficient strength to bear a weight not exceeding 40 pounds for a distance of from five to eight miles daily over fairly good ground.

half across the mud swamp, and yet saw no signs of the poor coolie, I was almost giving up my quest in despair, when my eye caught something moving about half a mile farther on. It was the goat all by itself. I made for it with a sinking heart.

It was only on getting quite close to it that I perceived the poor coolie, lying flat and half sunk in the mud. He had fallen in a faint, and though he was still breathing, he was quite insensible. Fortunately he had taken the precaution of tying the rope of the *rabbu* tight round his arm, and thus not only was it owing to the animal that I had found his whereabouts, but I had also saved our precious acquisition. With some rubbing and shaking I brought the poor fellow back to life, and supported him by the arm until we rejoined Chanden Sing. Not till the middle of the night did we reach Tarbar, a large Tibetan encampment at the foot of the hill range.

CHAPTER LXIX

THE alarm of our arrival, given first by scores of dogs barking at us, then by one of the natives who had ventured to leave his tent to find out the cause of the disturbance, created the usual panic in the place.

"*Gigri duk! gigri duk! Jogpa, Jogpa!*" (Danger, danger; help; brigands!) cried the Tibetan, running frantically out of his tent; and a few seconds later, black figures could be seen everywhere, rushing in and out of their tents in a state of confusion. It must be remembered that, according to the manners of Tibet, one should time one's arrival at an encampment so as to reach it before sundown, unless notice of one's approach is sent ahead. People who arrive unexpectedly in the middle of the night are never credited with good motives, and their appearance is associated with all sorts of evil intentions—murder, robbery, or extortion. I tried to set the minds of the good folk at ease, by stating that I meant no harm; but such were their excitement and confusion that I could get no one to listen to me.

Two old women came to us with a bucket of milk and laid it at my feet, entreating me to spare their lives; and great was their astonishment when, instead of finding themselves murdered, they received a silver rupee in payment. This was the first step towards a peaceful settlement of the disturbance. After some time, calm was

restored, and, though still regarded with considerable suspicion, we were politely treated by the natives.

Unfortunately, here too we were unable to purchase
provisions, the natives declaring that they had not sufficient for themselves. So, having feasted on the *rabbu*

CARPENTER AND SADDLE-MAKER

which we killed, and on yak's milk, we made preparations
to strike camp early next morning.

At night the thermometer fell to 26°, and the cold was
very great; but we purchased a quantity of dung from the
natives and made a fine fire in the morning; and, having
had a good meal after several days' privations, we felt
happier than usual. The natives begged as ever, show-

ing their unrestrained craving for money, to get which they would lower themselves to anything.

Northwest of the encampment, through a gorge, flowed a wide river which skirted the foot of the mountains. It was snow-fed, for in the evening the current was strong and deep, whereas early in the morning the level of the water was several feet lower, being, however, even then hardly fordable. On leaving Tarbar, we followed for a while the course of the river, and the day being glorious, we were able to admire fully the magnificent panorama of the great rugged mountain-range to our southwest. The higher peaks were nearly all of a pyramidical shape, and at 226 30 (b. m.) I observed a gigantic quadrangular peak which I took to be Mount Everest. Next to it, at 225 30 (b. m.), is a pyramidical peak, very lofty, but not to be compared in height or beauty to its neighbor. I followed a general course towards 120 (b.m.), and as the river, which we had more or less followed, now described a big bend towards the south-southeast, I decided to cross it. We waded through it successfully with water up to our necks, and again we found ourselves upon marshy land, with a repetition of the previous day's experience.

OLD WOMAN

Farther on we crossed three more tributaries of the larger stream, all fairly wide and deep; and then we had once more to get across the main river, now of such depth and rapidity as to cause us much trouble and no small danger. The river traverses the plain in zigzag fashion, and, unless we wanted to follow its banks, and so lengthen the journey by double or treble the distance, this was the only course open to us. Thus, while trying to travel in a straight line, we found ourselves for the third time confronted by this great river, now swollen by other snow-fed streams, and carrying an immense body of water. It was in the afternoon, too, when the water was at its highest. We attempted a crossing at several points, but found it impossible; so I made up my mind to wait for low water early next morning.

CHAPTER LXX

ANOTHER TIBETAN ENCAMPMENT — UNCONTROLLABLE ANIMALS—A BIG STREAM—WASHED AWAY — IN DREADFUL SUSPENSE—RESCUING THE YAK—DIVING AT GREAT ALTITUDES AND ITS EFFECTS — HOW MY TWO FOLLOWERS GOT ACROSS—A PRECARIOUS OUTLOOK AND A LITTLE COMFORT

APPARENTLY my yaks knew this part of the country well; and I noticed that, whenever I lost the track, all I had to do was to follow them, and they would bring me back to it again. Even when I drove them away from the track, they showed a great dis-inclination to move, whereas they proceeded willingly enough while we were on the high-road, which, mark you, is no road at all, for no track is visible except here and there, where the footprints of the last nomads, with their sheep, ponies, and yaks, have destroyed the grass.

CONTRIVANCE FOR CARRYING LOADS

Half a mile on the other side of the river was an encampment of some fifty or sixty tents, with hundreds of yaks, and sheep graz-ing near it.

At this point my two yaks, which I noticed had been marching with more than usual smartness, bolted while I was ordering Chanden Sing and Mansing to take down the loads, and went straight into the water.

In attempting to make them turn back, Mansing threw a stone at them, which, however, only sent them on all the faster. The current was so strong, and the bottom

of the river so soft, that they both sank, and when they
reappeared on the surface it was only to float rapidly
away down stream. We watched them with ever-increasing anxiety, for they seemed quite helpless. We ran
panting along the river bank, urging them on with shouts
to drive them to the other side. Alas, in their desperate

RESCUING A YAK

struggle to keep afloat, and powerless against the current, the two yaks collided violently in mid-stream, and
the bump caused the pack-saddle and loads of the smaller
yak to turn over. The animal, thus overbalanced and
hampered, sank and reappeared two or three times, struggling for air and life. It was, indeed, a terrible moment.
I threw off my clothes and jumped into the water. I
swam fast to the animal, and, with no small exertion,
pulled him on shore, some two hundred yards farther
down the stream. We were both safe, though breath-
less, but, alas! the ropes that held the baggage had given

way, and saddle and loads had disappeared. This loss
was a dreadful blow to us. I tried hard, by repeatedly
diving into the river, until I was almost frozen, to recover
my goods, but failed to find them, or even to locate them.
Where I suspected them to be the water was over twenty
feet deep, and the bottom of the river was of soft mud;
so that the weight of the loads would have caused them
to sink and be covered over with it.

Diving at such very great elevations gave one a peculiar and unpleasant sensation. The moment I was entirely under water, I felt as if I were compressed under
an appalling weight which seemed to crush me. Had
the liquid above and around me been a mass of lead instead of water, it could not have felt heavier. The sensation was especially noticeable in my head, which felt as
if my skull were being screwed into a vice. The beating
at my temples was so strong that, though in ordinary
circumstances I can remain under water for over a minute, I could there never hold out for longer than fifteen
or twenty seconds. Each time that I shot out from below, gasping for air, my heart beat alarmingly hard, and
my lungs seemed as if about to burst.

I was so exhausted that I did not feel equal to convey-
ing across my two men. So I unloaded the stronger
yak, and then, with endless fatigue, I drove him and his
mate again into the water. Unhampered, and good
swimmers as they are, they floated away with the current
and reached the other side. Chanden Sing and Mansing,
with his clothes and mine tied into a bundle over their
shoulders, got on the animals, and, after a somewhat anxious passage, they arrived safely on my side, where we
camped, my men mourning all night over the lost property. The next morning I made fresh attempts to recover
the loads, but in vain! Unhappily they contained all

my tinned provisions, and what little other food I had, and they had in them besides eight hundred rupees in silver, the greater part of my ammunition, changes of clothing and three pairs of shoes, my copper hurricane lantern, and sundry knives and razors.

The only thing we recovered was the pack-saddle, which was washed ashore some six hundred yards farther down. Our situation can be summed up in a few words. We were now in the centre of Tibet, with no food of any kind, no clothes to speak of, and no boots or shoes, except those we wore, which were falling to pieces. What little ammunition I had left could not be relied upon, owing to its having been in the water on several occasions; and round us we had nothing but enemies—insignificant enemies if you like, yet enemies for all that.

I got what comfort I could out of the knowledge that at least the water-tight cases with my scientific instruments, notes, sketches, and maps were saved, and as far as I was concerned, I valued them more than anything else I possessed.

CHAPTER LXXI

WE went on, hungry, worn out, with out feet lacerated, cheering one another as best we could. We laughed at our troubles; we laughed at the Tibetans and their comical ways; we laughed at everything and everybody, until eventually we even laughed at ourselves. When you are hungry, the sun seems slow at describing its daily semicircle from east to west; yet though involuntary fasting gives you at first an acute pain in the stomach, it doesn't become unbearable until after several days' absolute want of food; that is to say, if you are in a way accustomed, as we were, to extra long intervals between one meal and the next. When we got to our third day's fasting we were keen enough for a meal; and, perceiving some black tents close by the mountain side, about four miles out of our course, we made for them with hungry haste. We purchased two bucketsful of yak's milk, one of which I drank there and then myself, the second being equally divided between my two servants. That was all we could get. They would sell us absolutely nothing else.

After this we moved forward again, making steady, and, if one allows for the great elevation we were at, comparatively rapid progress; noting down everything, and holding our own against all comers. We encountered pleasant people, and some unpleasant ones, but, whether their manner was courteous or the reverse, we could nowhere obtain food for love or money.

Poor Mansing and Chanden Sing, not having the same interest that I had in my work to keep up their spirits, were now in a dreadful condition. Cold, tired, and starved,

MYSELF DRINKING OUT OF A BUCKET

the poor wretches had hardly strength left to stand on their feet, the soles of which were badly cut and very sore. It really made my heart bleed to see these two brave fellows suffer as they did for my sake; and yet no word of complaint came from them; not once did their lips utter a reproach.

"Never mind if we suffer or even die," said the poor

fellows, when I expressed my sympathy with them, "we will follow you as long as we have strength to move, and we will stand by you, no matter what happens."

I had to relieve Chanden Sing of his rifle, as he was no longer able to carry it. I myself, too, felt languid and exhausted as the days went by, and got scarcely any food. I cannot say that I experienced any very severe physical

SHRINE INSIDE TENT

pain. This was due, I think, to the fact that my exhaustion brought on fever. I had, nevertheless, a peculiar feeling in my head, as if my intellect, never too bright, had now been altogether dulled. My hearing, too, became less acute; and I felt my strength slowly dying down like the flame of a lamp with no more oil in it. The nervous excitement and strain alone kept me alive, and I went on walking mechanically.

92

CHAPTER LXXII

EIGHTY BLACK TENTS—STARVED—KINDLY NATIVES—PRESENTS—ANDO
AND HIS PROMISES—A FRIENDLY LAMA—A LOW PASS—MY PLANS

WE reached an encampment of some eighty black
tents and a mud guard-house. We were positively in a
starved condition and it was utterly impossible to proceed farther, owing to the wretched condition of my two
men. They begged to be given ponies to ride, for their
feet were so sore that, notwithstanding their anxiety to
follow me, they could not.

The natives received us very kindly, and, on my applying for them, consented to sell me ponies, clothes, and
provisions. We encamped about two miles beyond the
settlement, and during the evening several persons visited my tent, bringing gifts of flour, butter, and *tsamba*,
accompanied by *Katas*, the veils of friendship. I made a
point of invariably giving the Tibetans, in return for
their gifts, silver money to an amount three or four
times greater than the value of the articles they presented us with, and they professed to be very grateful for
it. A man called Ando, who styled himself a Gourkha,
but wore the garb of the Tibetans, came to visit us in
our tent, and promised to bring for sale several ponies
the next morning. He also undertook to sell me a sufficient quantity of food to enable us to reach Lhassa,
and, to show his good faith, brought a portion of the supplies in the evening, and said he would let us have the
remainder the next morning.

We next had a visit from a Lama, who appeared both
civil and intelligent, and who presented us with some butter and *chura* (cheese). He had travelled in India, he told
us, as far as Calcutta, and was on his way from Gartok to
Lhassa, where he expected to arrive in four or five days,

MUD GUARD-HOUSE.

having an excellent pony. Other Lamas and men who
came to see us stated that they had come from Lhassa in
that time, and I do not think that they can have been
far wrong, as the whole distance from the Lippu Pass on
the frontier (near Garbyang) to Lhassa can be covered in
sixteen days on horseback.

The natives, as usual, showed great reticence in letting
out the name of the encampment, some calling it Toxem,
others Taddju. North of us was a low pass in the hill
range, and it was my intention, if I succeeded in purchasing provisions and ponies, to cross over this pass

and proceed towards the Sacred City, following a course on the northern side of the mountain range, having already seen as much as I wanted of the Tibetans. Besides, the highway to Lhassa was getting so thickly populated that I thought it advisable to travel through less inhabited regions. I intended proceeding, dressed as a European, until within a few miles of Lhassa. Then I would leave my two men concealed in some secluded spot, and assuming a disguise, I would penetrate alone during the night into the city. This would have been easy

TIBETAN BELLOWS

enough, as Lhassa has no gates, and only a ruined wall round it.

I succeeded in purchasing some clothing and boots from the Tibetans, and the pigtail that I needed to make me pass for a Tibetan I intended to make myself, out of the silky hair of my yaks. To avoid betraying myself by my inability to speak Tibetan fluently, I thought of pretending to be deaf and dumb.

A good meal brought hope and high spirits, and when I retired to sleep I saw myself already inside the sacred walls.

II.—II

DURING the night I was aroused several times by noises, and I went out of my tent to look for the disturbers, but failed to discover any one. This had become my nightly experience, and I attached very little importance to these sounds.

In the morning, Ando and two or three Tibetans came to sell us provisions and ponies, and, while my two servants and I were engaged in purchasing what we required, I saw a number of villagers coming up in groups. Some spun their wool, others carried bags of *tsamba* and flour, while others still arrived leading a number of fine ponies. Having purchased provisions to last us a couple of months, we now began the selection of mounts, and naturally my servants and myself were overjoyed at our unexpected piece of luck in finding ourselves, after untold sufferings and privations of all kinds, confronted with abundance of everything we could possibly desire. The demeanor of the Tibetans was so friendly, and they seemed so guileless, that I never thought of suspecting them. Chanden Sing and Mansing, who at

A DISTAFF

PURCHASING PONIES

bottom were sportsmen of the very first order, delighted
at the prospect of getting animals, rode first one pony
and then another to suit themselves; and Chanden Sing,
having selected a handsome beast for his own use, called
me to try it and examine it before paying over the pur-
chase-money. Unsuspecting of foul play, and also because it would not be convenient to try the various lively
ponies with my rifle slung over my shoulder, I walked

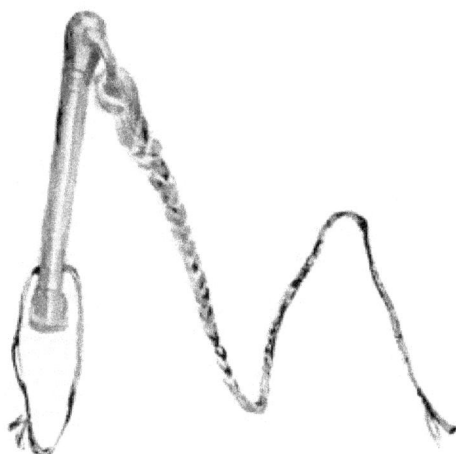

ROPE RIDING-WHIP

unarmed to the spot, about a hundred yards away from
my tent, where the restless animal was being held for my
inspection. The natives followed behind me, but such a
thing being common in any country when one buys a
horse in public, I thought nothing of it. As I stood with
my hands behind my back, I well recollect the expression
of delight on Chanden Sing's face when I approved of his
choice, and, as is generally the case on such occasions,
the crowd behind in a chorus expressed their gratuitous
opinion on the superiority of the steed selected. I had
just stooped to look at the pony's fore legs, when I was
suddenly seized from behind by several persons, who

I WAS A PRISONER

grabbed me by the neck, wrists, and legs, and threw me
down on my face. I struggled and fought until I shook
off some of my assailants and regained my feet; but

others rushed up, and I was surrounded by some thirty
men, who attacked me from every side, and clinging to
me with all their might succeeded in grabbing my arms,
legs and head. Weak as I was, they knocked me down
three more times, and three more times I regained my
feet. I fought to the bitter end with my fists, feet, head,
and teeth each time that I got one hand or leg free from
their clutches, hitting right and left at any part where I
could disable my opponents. Their timidity, even when
in such overwhelming numbers, was indeed beyond description; and it was entirely due to it, and not to my
strength (for I had hardly any), that I was able to hold
my own against them for some twenty minutes. My
clothes were torn to bits in the fight. Long ropes were
thrown at me from every side, and I became so entangled
in them that my movements were impeded. One rope
which they flung and successfully twisted round my neck
completed their victory. They pulled hard at it from the
two ends, and while I panted and gasped with the exertion of fighting, they tugged and tugged to strangle me,
till I felt as if my eyes would shoot out of their sockets.
I was suffocating. My sight became dim, and I was in
their power. Dragged down to the ground, they stamped,
and kicked, and trampled upon me with their heavy nailed
boots, until I was stunned. Then they tied my wrists
tightly behind my back; they bound my elbows, my
chest, my neck and my ankles. I was a prisoner!

CHAPTER LXXIV

THEY lifted me and made me stand up. The brave Chanden Sing had been struggling with all his might against fifteen or twenty foes, and had disabled several of them. He had been pounced upon at the same moment that I was, and had fought gallantly until, like myself, he had been entangled, thrown down and secured by ropes. During my struggle I heard him call out repeatedly: "*Banduk, banduk, Mansing; jaldi banduk!*" (Rifle, rifle, Mansing; quick, my rifle!) but, alas, poor Mansing the leper, the weak and jaded coolie, had been sprung upon by four powerful Tibetans, who held him pinned to the ground as if he had been the fiercest of bandits. Mansing was a philosopher. He had saved himself the trouble of even offering any resistance; but he, too, was illtreated and beaten and tightly bound. At the beginning of the fight a shrill whistle had brought up four hundred* armed soldiers who had lain in

EAR-RING WORN BY HIGH OFFICIALS

*The Lamas stated afterwards that this was the number.

CRAMMED INTO THE SETTLEMENT

ambush round us, concealed behind the innumerable sand-
hills and in the depressions in the ground. They took up
a position round us and covered us with their matchlocks.

All was now over, and, bound like a dangerous criminal,
I looked round to see what had become of my men. When
I realised that it took the Tibetans five hundred men*
all counted to arrest a starved Englishman and his two
half-dying servants, and that, even then, they dared not do
it openly, but had to resort to abject treachery; when I
found that these soldiers were picked troops from Lhassa
and Sigatz (Shigatze), despatched on purpose to arrest
our progress and capture us, I could not restrain a smile
of contempt for those into whose hands we had at last
fallen.

My blood boiled when, upon the order of the Lama,
who the previous night had professed to be our friend,
several men advanced and searched our pockets. They
rifled us of everything we possessed, and began overhauling our baggage. The watches and chronometer were
looked upon with suspicion, their ticking causing anxiety
and curiosity. They were passed round and round and
mercilessly thrown about from one person to the other,
until they stopped. They were then pronounced "dead."
The compasses and aneroids, which they could not distinguish from watches, were soon thrown aside, as "they
had no life in them," but great caution was displayed in
touching our rifles, which were lying on our bedding
when the tent had been torn down.

Great fears were entertained lest they should go off by
themselves; and it was only on my assurance (which
made our captors ten times more cautious) that they were
not loaded, that at last they took them and registered

---

* Counting Lamas, villagers, and soldiers.

them in the catalogue of our confiscated property. I had upon me a gold ring that my mother had given me when I was a child. I asked permission to retain it, and with their superstitious nature they immediately thought that it had occult powers, like the wands one reads of in fairy tales.

A man called Nerba, who later on played an important part in our sufferings, was intrusted with it, and warned never to let me see it again. As we three prisoners sat bound and held down by guards it was heartbreaking to see the Lamas and officers handle all our things so roughly as to spoil nearly all they touched; but particularly disgusting was their avidity when, in searching the pockets of the coat I wore daily, and which I had not put on that morning, they found a quantity of silver coins, some eight hundred rupees in all. Officers, Lamas, and soldiers made a grab for the money, and when order was re-established only a few coins remained where the sum had been laid down. Other moneys which they found in one of our loads met with a similar fate. Among the things arousing greatest curiosity was an india-rubber pillow fully blown out. The soft, smooth texture of the india-rubber seemed to catch their fancy, and one after the other they rubbed their cheeks on the cushion, exclaiming at the pleasant sensation it gave them. However, in playing with the brass screw by which the cushion is inflated, they gave it a turn, and the imprisoned air found its way out with a hissing noise. This created quite a panic among the Tibetans, and many were the conjectures of their superstitious minds as to the mean-

A SPEAR

ing of the strange contrivance. They regarded it as an evil omen, and naturally I took advantage of any small incident of this kind to work judiciously on their superstitions and frighten them as much as I could.

TIBETANS OVERHAULING OUR BAGGAGE

The Tibetans, having examined all except my watertight cases of instruments, photographic plates, and sketches, seemed so upset at one or two things that happened, and at some remarks I made, that they hurriedly sealed up all my property in bags and blankets, and ordered the things to be placed on yaks and brought into the guard-house of the settlement. This done, they tied the end of the ropes that bound our necks to the pommels of their saddles, and, having loosed our feet, they sprang on their ponies and rode off, with shouts, hisses, and cries of victory, firing their matchlocks in the air, and dragging us prisoners into the settlement.

CHAPTER LXXV

ON reaching the settlement, my last words to my men before we were separated were: " No matter what they do to you, do not let them see that you suffer," and they promised to obey me. We were then conveyed to different tents. I was dragged to one of the larger tents, inside and outside of which soldiers were placed on guard. Those near me were at first sulky and rough in their manner and speech, but I always made a point of answering them in as collected and polite a fashion as I could. I had on many previous occasions found that nothing carries one further in dealings with Asiatics than to keep calm and cool, and I saw in a moment that if we were ever to get out of our present scrape it would be by maintaining a perfectly impassive demeanor in face of anything that might take place. Whether I acted my part well it is not for me to say, but the reader can satisfy himself on that point by perusing the Government inquiry and report made by Mr. J. Larkin, and given in the Appendix to this book.

The tent being kept closed, I was unable to discover what happened outside, but from the noises I heard of people rushing hither and thither, and of shouted orders, besides the continuous tinkling of the soldiers' horse-bells as they galloped past the tent, I concluded that the place must be in a state of turmoil. I had been some three hours in the tent when a soldier entered and ordered me out.

"They are going to cut off his head," said he to his comrades; and, turning round to me, he made a significant gesture with his hand across his neck.

"*Nikutza*" (All right), said I, dryly.

It must not be forgotten that when a Tibetan himself hears words of this import, he usually goes down on his

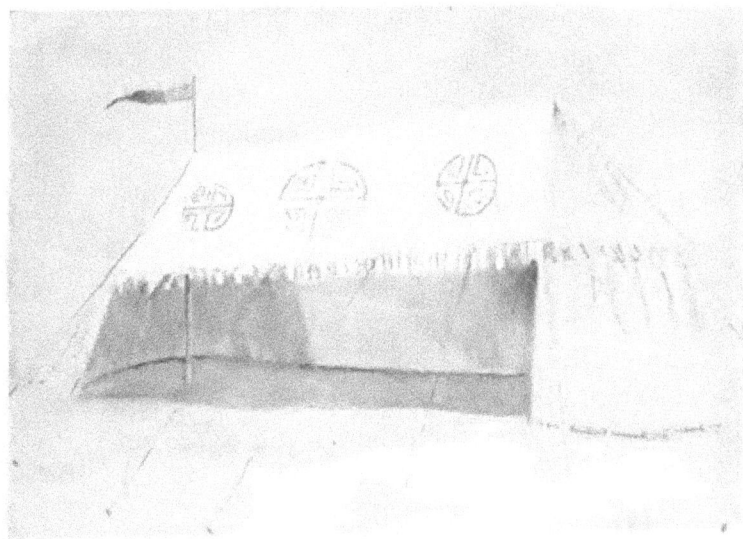

THE POMBO'S TENT

knees and implores to be spared, with tears, and sobs, and prayers in profusion. So it is not surprising that the Tibetans were somewhat astonished at my answer, and seemed puzzled as to what to make of it. Anyhow, the first ardor of the messenger was sensibly cooled down, and I was led out with more reluctance than firmness.

During the time I had been shut up, a huge white tent with blue ornaments had been pitched in front of the mud-house, and round it were hundreds of soldiers and villagers—a most picturesque sight.

As I was led nearer, I perceived that the front of the tent was wide open, and inside stood a great number of red Lamas, with shaven heads, in their long woollen tunics. The soldiers stopped me when I was about twenty yards from the tent. Additional ropes were added to those already cutting into my wrists, elbows, and chest, and the others made tighter. I perceived Chanden Sing led forward, and then, instead of taking me before the Lamas, they pushed me to the rear of the solitary mud-house to preclude my witnessing the scene that followed. I heard Chanden Sing being interrogated in a loud, angry tone of voice, and accused of having been my guide. Next I heard wild shouts from the crowd, then a dead silence. A few instants later I distinguished the snapping noise of a lash, followed by hoarse moans from my poor bearer, to whom they were evidently applying it.

I counted the strokes, the sickening noise of which is still well impressed on my memory, as they regularly and steadily fell one after the other to twenty, to thirty, forty, and fifty. Then there was a pause.

CHAPTER LXXVI

A NUMBER of soldiers now came for me, and I was first led, then pushed violently before the tribunal.

On a high seat in the centre of the tent sat a man wearing ample trousers of gaudy yellow and a short yellow coat with flowing sleeves. On his head he had a huge four-pointed hat, gilt all over, and with three great eyes painted on it. He was young-looking, and his head was clean shaven, as he was a Lama of the highest order, a Grand Lama and a *Pombo*, or Governor of the province, with powers equivalent to those of a feudal king. On his right stood a stout and powerful red Lama who held a huge double-handed sword, and behind, and at the sides, were a number of other Lamas, officers and soldiers. As I stood silent, and with my head held high before him, two or three Lamas rushed at me and ordered me to kneel. They tried to compel me to do so, by forcing me on my knees, but I succeeded in maintaining an upright posture.

The Pombo, who was furious at my declining to kneel before him, addressed me in words that sounded violent; but as he spoke classical Tibetan, and I only the colloquial language, I could not understand a word of what he said, and I meekly asked him not to use such fine words, as they were unintelligible to me.

The great man was taken aback at this unheard-of request, and, with a frown on his face, he pointed to me to look to my left. The soldiers and Lamas drew aside, and I beheld Chanden Sing lying flat on his face, stripped from the waist downward, in front of a row of Lamas and military men. Two powerful Lamas, one on each side of him, began again to castigate him with knotted leather thongs weighted with lead, laying on their strokes with vigorous arms from his waist to his feet. He was bleeding all over. Each time that a lash fell on his wounded skin it felt as if a dagger had been stuck into my chest; but I knew Orientals too well to show any pity for the man, as this would have only involved a more severe punishment for him. So I looked on at his torture as one would upon a thing of every-day occurrence. The Lamas nearer to me shook their fists under my nose, and explained that my turn would come next, whereupon I smiled and repeated the usual "*Nikutza, nikutza*" (Very good, very good).

The Pombo and his officers were at a loss what to

THE POMBO

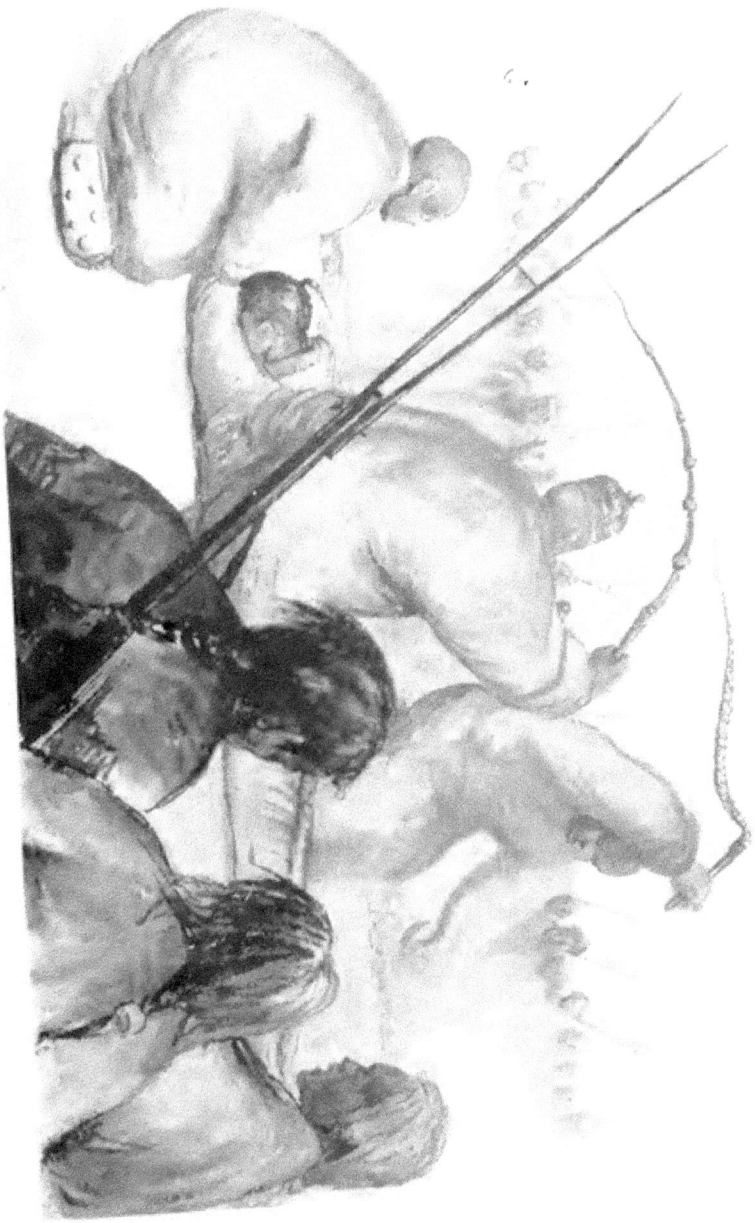

CHANDEN SING BEING FLOGGED

make of me, as I could plainly see by their faces; so that the more I perceived how well my plan was answering, the more courage I screwed up to play my part to the best of my ability.

The Pombo, an effeminate, juvenile, handsome person, almost hysterical in manner, and likely to make a splendid subject for hypnotic experiments (I had reason to think, indeed, that he had already often been under mesmeric influence), remained with his eyes fixed upon mine as if in a trance for certainly over two minutes.

There was a wonderful and sudden change in the man, and his voice, arrogant and angry a few moments before, was now soft and apparently kindly. The Lamas around him were evidently concerned at seeing their lord and master transformed from a foaming fury to the quietest of lambs; so they seized me and brought me out of his sight to the spot where Chanden Sing was being chastised. Here again, I could not be compelled to kneel, so at last I was allowed to squat down before the Pombo's officers.

CHAPTER LXXVII

THE two Lamas, leaving Chanden Sing, produced my
note-books and maps, and proceeded to interrogate me

A SOLDIER

closely, saying that, if I spoke the truth, I should be
spared, otherwise I should be flogged and then beheaded.

I answered that I would speak the truth, whether they
punished me or not.

One of the Lamas, a great big brute, who was dressed up in a gaudy red silk coat, with gold embroidery at the collar, and who had taken part in the flogging of Chanden Sing, told me I must say "that my servant had shown me the road across Tibet, and that he had done the maps and sketches." If I would say this, they were willing to release me and have me conveyed back to the frontier, promising to do me no further harm. They would cut my servant's head off, that was all, but no personal injury should be inflicted on me.

I explained clearly to the Lamas that I alone was responsible for the maps and sketches, and for finding my way so far inland. I repeated several times, slowly and distinctly, that my ser-

SOLDIER WITH PIGTAIL WOUND ROUND HIS HEAD

vant was innocent, and that therefore there was no reason to punish him. He had only obeyed my orders in following me to Tibet, and I alone, not my two servants, was to be punished if anybody was punishable.

The Lamas were angry at this, and one of them struck me violently on the head with the butt-end of his riding-crop. I pretended not to notice it, though it made my scalp ache and smart.

"Then we shall beat you and your man until you say what we want," the Lama exclaimed, angrily.

"You can beat us if you like," I replied with assurance, "but if you punish us unjustly it will go against yourselves. You can tear our skin off, and you can make us bleed to death, but you cannot make us feel pain."

Ando, the traitor, who spoke Hindustani fluently, acted as an interpreter whenever there was a hitch in our Tibetan conversation, and with what I knew of the language, and with this man's help, everything was explained to the Tibetans as clearly as possible. Notwithstanding this, they continued mercilessly to lash my poor servant, who, in his agony, was biting the ground as each blow fell on him and tore away patches of skin and flesh. Chanden Sing behaved heroically. Not a word of complaint, nor a prayer for mercy, came from his lips. He said that he had spoken the truth and had nothing more to say.

AN OFFICER

Watched intently by all the Lamas and soldiers, I sat with affected stoicism before this scene of cruelty, until, angry at my phlegm, order was given to the soldiers that I should be dragged away. Again they led me behind the mud-house, from where I could distinctly hear the angry cries of the Lamas cross-examining Chanden Sing, and those dreadful sounds of the lash still being administered.

It began to rain heavily, and this was a bit of luck for us, for in Tibet, as in China, a shower has a great effect upon the people, and even massacres have

been known to be put a stop to until the rain should
cease.

Such was the case that day. The moment the first
drops fell, the soldiers and Lamas rushed here, there, and
everywhere inside the tents, and I was hastily dragged
to the most distant tent of the settlement, which became
packed with the guards into whose charge I had been
given.

CHAPTER LXXVIII

An officer of high rank was sitting cross-legged at the farther end of the tent. He wore a handsome dark-red gown trimmed with gold and leopard skin, and was shod with tall black and red leather boots of Chinese shape. A beautiful sword with solid silver sheath inlaid with large pieces of coral and malachite was passed through his belt.

PURSE

This man, apparently between fifty and sixty years of age, had an intelligent, refined, honest, good-natured face; and somehow or other I felt from the very first moment I saw him that he would be a friend. And, indeed, whereas the soldiers and Lamas treated me with brutality and took every mean advantage that they could, this officer was alone in showing

FLINT AND
STEEL

some deference to me and some appreciation of my behavior. He made room by his side and signed that I might sit there.

SNUFFBOX

"I am a soldier," said he, in a dignified tone, "not a Lama. I have come from Lhassa with my men to arrest you, and you are now our prisoner. But you have shown no fear, and I respect you."

So saying, he inclined his head and laid his forehead

114

touching mine, and pulled out his tongue. Then he made a gesture signifying that, though he wished to, he could not then say more, owing to the presence of the soldiers.

Later on we entered into a most amicable conversation, in the course of which he said that he was a Rupun (a grade below that of general). I tried to explain to him all about English soldiers and weapons, and he displayed the keenest interest in all I told him. In return he gave me interesting information about the soldiers of Tibet. Every man in Tibet is considered a soldier in time of war or when required to do duty, but for the regular army all lads that are strong and healthy can enlist from the age of seventeen, those deformed or weakly being rejected as unfit for service. Good horsemanship is one of the qualities most appreciated in the Tibetan soldier, and, after that, unbounded obedience. The Rupun swore by the Tibetan matchlocks, which he believed to be the most serviceable weapons on earth; for, according to him, as long as you had powder enough, you could use anything as a missile. Pebbles, earth, or nails did as good work as any lead bullet.

FLINT-AND-STEEL POUCH

He told me that large quantities of these weapons were manufactured at Lhassa and Sigatz (Shigatze), and he stated that the majority of Tibetan men outside the towns possess one. Gunpowder was also made with saltpetre and sulphur found in the country.

The Rupun, seeing how quick I was at picking up words, took a special delight in teaching me, as one would a child, the names of the several grades in the Tibetan army. The *Tchu-pun** was the lowest grade, and only had ten men under him; then came the *Kiatsamba-pun* or *Kia-pun,†* or officer in command of one hundred soldiers; and the *Tung-pun,‡* or head of one thousand. These officers, however, are seldom allowed the full com-

plement of soldiers according to their grade, and very often the "commander of one thousand" has only under him three or four hundred men at the most. Above the *Tung-pun* comes the *Rupun*, a kind of adjutant-general; then the *Dah-pun*, or great officer; and highest of all, the *Mag-pun* (or *Mag-bun*, as it is usually pronounced), the general in chief.

The acquaintance of one of these generals we had already made at Gyanema. Though my informant said that officers are elected for their bravery in time of war and for their strength and aptitude in the saddle and with their weapons, I knew well enough that such was not the case. The posts are mainly given to whoever can afford to pay most for them, and to men of families under special protection of the Lamas. In many cases they are actually sold by auction.

LEATHER HORSE- WHIP

The method described by the Rupun was nevertheless what is popularly believed by the masses of Tibet to be the way in which military officers are chosen.

Tchu, ten, *pun*, officer, or officer of ten men.
† *Kiatsamba* or *Kia* = one hundred.
‡ *Tung* = one thousand.

CHAPTER LXXIX

THE Rupun possessed a good deal of dry humor, and
I told him how fast the Tibetan soldiers had run away
on previous occasions when I had met them and had my
rifle by me. But he was quite equal to the situation and
exclaimed: "Yes, I know that they ran, but it was not
through fear. It was because they did not wish to hurt
you." Upon which I answered that, if that were the
case, they need not have run so fast.

The Rupun seemed amused and laughed at my sar-
casm. He patted me on the back and said I was right.
He professed to be grieved to see me tied up, and said
he had received strict orders not to give me food or unloose my bonds.

The soldiers, who had been listening open-mouthed to
the affable and friendly conversation between the Rupun
and myself, a practice not common in Tibet between
captor and prisoner, followed their chief's example, and
from being harsh and rough, turned quite kindly and
respectful. They placed a cushion under me and tried
to make me as comfortable as they could in the circumstances.

Towards the evening, however, the Rupun was summoned before the Pombo, and the guard was relieved by
a fresh lot of men. This was a change for the worse.
Their manner was extremely rough, and they dragged

117

me away from the dignified seat I had occupied in the place of honor in the tent, and knocked me violently down on a heap of dung which they used for fuel.

"That is the place for *plenkis!*" shouted one of the men, "not in the best part of the tent."

They pounced upon me roughly, and though I made no resistance whatever, they again tied my feet together, and another rope was fastened round my knees. The ends of these ropes were left long, and each was given in charge of a soldier.

No part of a Tibetan tent is over clean, but the spot where I was to rest for the night was the dirtiest. Bound so tightly that the ropes cut channels in my flesh, it was out of the question to sleep; but tenfold worse than this was the disgusting fact that I soon got covered with vermin, which swarmed in the tent. From this time till the end of my captivity, or twenty-five days later, I suffered unspeakable tortures from this pest. The guards, with their swords drawn, were all round me inside the tent, and other were posted outside.

CHARM-BOX

The night was full of strange events. Shouts could be heard at intervals from a distance outside, and some one of the guard in the tent answered them. They were to keep the men awake and make sure that I was still there. One of the soldiers in the tent revolved his

A PRAYER

prayer-wheel, muttering the following prayer so often
that I learned it by heart:

Sangbo, sangbo
Yabni namla dupehenché
Yumni sala lockchendir
Lashin shukpi Kani san
Pashin tagpe Kani san
Yulo parba palui san
Tumlo parba wumboi san
Lassan lussan tamjeh san
Chedan Kordan jindan san
Takpeh yeiki polloh san
Takpeh yonki molloh san
Tzurzu Kaghi Tablah san
Arah, Banza, Nattitti
Jehmi jangla changzalu.

The almost literal translation of the words is this:

Oh, my God, I confess
That my father has gone to heaven,
But my mother is at present alive (*lit.* in the house).
First my mother sinned
And you took all men to heaven,
Then my mother and father sinned and I will go to heaven.
If all other men and I sin, and we withdraw our sins,
We are all liable to sin and the wumboo wood absolves (*lit.* washes all)
    from all sins.
On the northwest (Lassan) and southeast (Lussan) are the two ways
    to heaven.
I read the holy book and purify myself,
My arm-bone* is the sacred bone (*lit.* God's bone).
And the sign of manhood my left arm.
Oh, my God, who art above my head,
And at the sacred Kujernath, Banzah and Nattitti,
I pray every day for health and wealth (silver and gold).

* The Tibetans believe that in men the left, and in women the right, arm
belongs to God. They regard it as sacred, because with this arm food is
conveyed to the mouth, thus giving life to the body, and also because it is
with the arms that one can defend oneself against one's enemies. The
bone of the nose is also regarded as sacred.

119

In the middle of the night the Rupun returned. I noticed he seemed very much upset. He sat by my side,
and by the light of the flickering fire and a wick burning

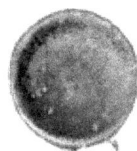

PUKU, OR
WOODEN CUP

in a brass bowl filled with butter, I could
see in his face an expression of great anxiety. I felt, by the compassionate way in
which he looked at me, that he had grave
news to give me. I was not mistaken. He
moved me from the pestilent place where
I had been thrown down helpless by the
soldiers, and laid me in a more comfortable and cleaner
part of the tent. Then he ordered a soldier to bring
me a blanket. Next, to my astonishment, he became
very severe, and said he must examine my bonds. He
turned quite angry, scolding the soldiers for leaving me
so insecurely tied, and proceeded to make
the knots firmer, a thing which I felt was
impossible. Though he pretended to use
all his strength in doing this, I found, much
to my amazement, that my bonds were really becoming loosened. He then quickly
covered me up with the blanket.

PUKU, OR
WOODEN CUP

The soldiers were at the other end of the
large tent, and seemed occupied with a loud argument
over some paltry matter. The Rupun, stooping low,

and making pretence to tuck me in the blanket, whispered:

"Your head is to be cut off to-morrow. Escape to-night. There are no soldiers outside."

The good man was actually preparing everything for my flight. He put out the light, and came to sleep by my side. It would have been comparatively easy, when all the men had fallen asleep, to slip from under the tent and steal away. I had got my hands easily out of the ropes, and should have had no difficulty in undoing all my other bonds; but the thought that I should be leaving my two men at the mercy of the Tibetans prevented my carrying the escape into effect. The Rupun, having risen to see that the guard were asleep, lay down again close to me and murmured:

"*Nelon, nelon ; paladö*" (They are asleep; go).

Well meant and tempting as the offer was, I told him I must stay with my men.

Having my hands free, I managed to sleep a little during the night; and when the morning came I slipped my hands again inside the ropes.

The Rupun, who seemed much disappointed, tied the ropes round my wrists firmly again, and though he appeared rather vexed at my not having availed myself of the chance of flight he had given me, he treated me with ever-increasing respect and deference. He even produced his *puku* (wooden bowl), which he filled with steaming tea from the *raksang*,* and lifted it up to my mouth for me to drink.

On perceiving how thirsty and hungry I was, not only did this good man refill the cup time after time until my

---

* *Raksang*, a vessel in which tea mixed with butter and salt is kept boiling over the fire.

thirst was quenched, but he mixed with it *tsamba*, and lumps of butter, which he then stuffed into my mouth with his finger.

It was really touching to see how, moved to kindness, the soldiers imitated his example, and, one after the other, produced handfuls of *tsamba* and *chura*, and deposited them in my mouth. Their hands, it is true, were not over clean, but on such occasions it does not do to be too particular, and I was so hungry that the food they gave me seemed delicious. I had been for two nights and one day without food, and, what with the exertion of the fight and my various exciting experiences, my appetite was very keen.

This great politeness, however, and the sympathy with which not only the Rupun but even the soldiers treated me now, made me suspect that my end was indeed near. I was grieved not to be able to obtain news of Chanden Sing and Mansing; and the soldiers' reticence in answering questions regarding them made me fear that something awful had happened. Nevertheless, though my jailers were friendly, I did not betray any anxiety, but pretended to take all that came as a matter of course. I spent the first portion of the day in a lively conversation with the soldiers, partly to divert my thoughts and partly to improve my knowledge of Tibetan.

CHAPTER LXXXI

A BEARER OF BAD NEWS—MARCHED OFF TO THE MUD-HOUSE—MANSING
—INSULTS AND HUMILIATIONS—IRON HANDCUFFS INSTEAD OF ROPES
—THE RUPUN'S SYMPATHY—NO MORE HOPE—IN THE HANDS OF THE
MOB

EARLY in the afternoon a soldier entered the tent, and
striking me on the shoulder with his heavy hand, shouted :

"*Ohe!*" (This is a Tibetan exclamation always used
by the rougher classes when beginning a conversation. It
corresponds to " Look here.")

" *Ohe!*" repeated he ; " before the sun goes down you
will be flogged, both your legs will be broken,* they will
burn out your eyes, and then they will cut off your head!"

The man, who seemed quite in earnest, accompanied
each sentence with an appropriate gesture illustrating his
words. I laughed at him and affected to treat the whole
thing as a joke, partly because I thought this was the best
way to frighten them and prevent them from using vio-
lence, and partly because the programme thus laid before
me seemed so extensive that I thought it could only be
intended to intimidate me.

However, the words of the soldier cast a gloom over my
friendly guard in the tent, and when I tried to cheer them
up they answered bluntly that I would not laugh for very
long. Something was certainly happening, for the men
rushed in and out of the tent, and whispered among them-

---

* A form of torture in which, after placing the legs upon two parallel
logs of wood, a heavy blow is given with a mallet, fracturing both legs.

selves. When I spoke to them they would answer no more, and on my insisting, they made signs that their lips must from now be closed.

About half an hour later another person rushed into the tent in a great state of excitement, and signalled to my guards to lead me out. This they did, after making my

SOLDIER LAYING BEFORE ME THE PROGRAMME OF TORTURES

bonds tighter than ever, and placing extra ropes round my chest and arms. In this fashion I was marched off to the mud-house and led into one of the rooms. A large number of soldiers and villagers assembled outside, and after we had waited some time, Mansing, tightly bound, was brought into the same room. My pleasure at seeing my man again was so great that I forgot all about what was happening, and paid no attention to the insults of the mob peeping through the door. After a while a Lama came in with a smiling face and said he had good news to give me.

"We have ponies here," he said, "and we are going to take you back to the frontier, but the Pombo wishes to see you first to-day. Do not make any resistance. Let us exchange the ropes round your wrists for these iron handcuffs."

MY HANDCUFFS

Here he produced a heavy pair of them, which he had kept concealed under his coat.

"You will not wear them for more than a few moments, while we are leading you to his presence. Then you will be free. We swear to you by the Sun and Kunjuk-Sum that we will treat you kindly."

I promised not to resist, chiefly because I had no chance of doing so. For greater safety they tied my legs and placed a sliding knot round my neck; then I was carried out into the open, where a ring of soldiers with drawn swords stood round me. While I lay flat on my face on the ground, held down firmly, they unwound the ropes from around my wrists, and the iron fetters, joined by a heavy chain, were substituted for them. They took some time in fastening the clumsy padlock, after which, all being ready, they unbound my legs.

They made me stand up again, and knowing that I could not possibly get my hands free, they began to load me with insults and offensive terms, not directed to me as an individual, but as a *Plenki*, an Englishman. They spat upon me and threw mud at me. The Lamas behaved worse than any of the others, and the one who had sworn that I should be in no way ill-used if I would submit quietly to be handcuffed was the most prominent among my tormentors and the keenest in urging the crowd on to further brutality.

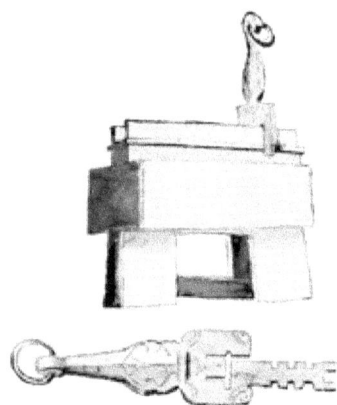

PADLOCK AND KEY

Suddenly the attention of the crowd was drawn to the approach of the Rupun with a number of soldiers and officers. He seemed depressed, and his face was of a ghastly yellowish tint. He kept his eyes fixed on the ground, and, speaking very low, ordered that I should again be conveyed inside the mud-house.

A few moments later he came in and closed the door after him, having first cleared the room of all the people who were in it. As I have mentioned before, Tibetan structures of this kind have a square aperture in the ceiling by which they are ventilated and lighted.

The Rupun laid his forehead upon mine in sign of compassion, and then sadly shook his head.

"There is no more hope," he whispered; "your head will be cut off to-night. The Lamas are bad and my heart is aching. You are like my brother, and I am grieved. . . ."

The good old man tried not to let me see his emotion, and made signs that he could stay no longer, lest he should be accused of being my friend.

The mob again entered the room, and I was once more dragged out into the open by the Lamas and soldiers. Some discussion followed as to who should keep the key of my handcuffs, and eventually it was handed over to one of the officers, who mounted his pony and rode away at a great rate in the direction of Lhassa.

TIBETAN HUT

CHAPTER LXXXII

Just then I heard the voice of my servant Chanden
Sing calling to me in a weak, agonized tone:

"*Hazur, Hazur, hum murgiaega!*" (Sir, sir, I am dying!) and, turning my head in the direction from which
these painful sounds came, I perceived my faithful bearer
with his hands bound behind his back, dragging himself
on his stomach towards the door of one of the other
rooms of the mud-house. His poor face was hardly
recognizable, it bore the traces of such awful suffering.

I could stand no more. Pushing my guards aside with
my shoulders, I endeavored to get to the poor wretch,
and had nearly reached him when the soldiers who stood
by sprang upon me, grappling me, and lifting me bodily
off my feet. They threw me on the back of a pony.

Though I now feared the worst, I tried to encourage
my brave servant by shouting to him that I was being
taken to Taklakot, and that he would be brought after
me the following day. He had exhausted his last atom
of strength in creeping to the door. He was roughly
seized, and brutally hurled back into the room of the
mud-house, so that we could not exchange a word more.
Mansing the coolie was placed with his arms pinioned
on a bare-backed pony. The saddle of the pony I had
been thrown upon is worthy of description. It was in

reality the wooden frame of a very high-backed saddle, from the back of which some five sharp iron spikes stuck out horizontally. As I sat on this implement of torture, the spikes caught me in the small of my back.

My guard having been augmented by twenty or thirty mounted men with muskets and swords, we set off at a

"SIR, SIR, I AM DYING!"

furious pace. A horseman riding in front of me led my pony by means of a cord, as my hands were manacled behind my back; and thus we travelled across country for miles.

But for those awful spikes in the saddle, the ride would not have been so very bad, for the pony I rode was a fine spirited animal, and the country around was curious and interesting. We proceeded along an apparently endless succession of yellow sand-hills, some of them as high as two or three hundred feet, others not more than twenty or thirty. The sand seemed to have been deposited more by wind than by water, though it is also possible that the whole basin, not very high above the level of the huge stream, may at some time have been altogether under water. The whole space between the mountain-range to the north of the Brahmaputra and the river itself was covered with these sand-mounds, except in certain places where the soil was extremely marshy, and where our ponies sank in deep soft mud. We splashed across sev-

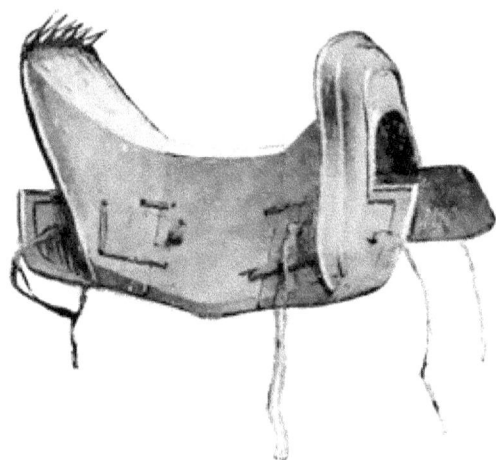

SPIKED SADDLE

eral rivulets and skirted a number of ponds. From the summit of a hill to which they led me I could see that the hills were of much greater circumference and height near the river edge, becoming smaller and smaller as they approached the mountain-range to the north. Moreover, they increased in number and size the farther we went in an easterly direction.

The circumstances under which I was now travelling did not permit me to ascertain the quality of the sand, or make any accurate investigations as to where the sand came from, but a glance at the country all round made me feel sure that the sand had been conveyed there from the south. This one could plainly see from depressions and wavelike undulations, showing that it had travelled (roughly) in a northerly direction; and although, having been unable to ascertain this for a fact, I do not wish to be too certain with regard to the movements and sources of these sand deposits, I was pretty firmly convinced that the sand had been deposited there by the wind, which had carried it over the Himahlyan chain from the plains of India.

My guard scoured the country from the high point of vantage to which we had ascended. Away in the distance, to the east, we saw a large number of horsemen raising clouds of dust; and riding down the hill, the ponies sinking in the soft sand, we set off in the direction of the newcomers, the surface at the bottom of the hill being more compact and harder.

CHAPTER LXXXIII

AT AN UNPLEASANT PACE—DRAWING NEAR THE CAVALCADE—A PIC-
TURESQUE SIGHT—A SHOT FIRED AT ME—TERRIBLE EFFECTS OF THE
SPIKES ALONG MY SPINE—THE ROPE BREAKS—AN ILL OMEN—A SEC-
OND SHOT MISSES ME—ARROWS—THE END OF MY TERRIBLE RIDE

WE travelled mile after mile at an unpleasant pace,
until we arrived at a spot where, drawn up in a line, was
the cavalcade we had seen from the summit of the hill.
It was a beautiful sight as we approached it, though the
pain which I was undergoing rather detracted from the
pleasure I should otherwise have taken in the picturesque
scene. There were about a hundred red Lamas in the
centre, with bannermen whose heads were covered by
peculiar flat fluffy hats, and the same number of soldiers
and officers in their gray, red, and black tunics; some two
hundred horsemen in all.

The Pombo, in his yellow coat and trousers and his
queer pointed hat, sat on a magnificent pony a little in
front of the crowd of Lamas and soldiers.

Curiously enough, when close to this new crowd, the
horseman who led my pony let go the rope, and the pony
was lashed cruelly and left to its own devices. The soldiers of my guard reined up and drew aside. The pony
dashed off in the direction of the Pombo, and as I passed
close to him a man named Nerba (private secretary of
the Tokchim Tarjum) knelt down, and, taking aim with
his matchlock resting on its prop, deliberately fired a shot
at me.

Although (I learned afterwards) this Nerba was one of

the champion shots in the country, and the distance from
the muzzle of his matchlock to me not more than four
yards, the bullet missed me, whizzing past my left ear.
Probably the speed at which my animal was proceeding
saved me, as the marksman could not take a very steady
aim; but my pony, startled at the sudden report of the
matchlock at such close quarters, took fright, and began

NERBA FIRING AT ME

rearing and plunging. I managed to maintain my seat,
though the spikes in the saddle were lacerating the lower
part of my spine terribly.

Several horsemen now rode up and captured my pony,
and preparations were made for another exciting number
in the programme of my tortures. In their way these
noble Lamas were of a sporting nature, but I swore to
myself that, no matter what they did to me, I would not
give them the satisfaction of seeing that they were hurt-
ing me. Acting on this principle, I pretended not to feel

the effect of the spikes tearing the flesh off my backbone;
and when they led me before the Pombo to show him how
covered with blood I was, I expressed satisfaction at riding such an excellent pony. This seemed to puzzle
them.

A cord of yak's hair, about forty or fifty yards long, was
now produced, the swivel attached to one end of it fastened to my handcuffs, and the other end held by a horseman. We set off again on our wild career, this time followed not only by the guard, but by the Pombo and all
his men. Once or twice I could not help turning round
to see what they were about. The cavalcade was a weird
and picturesque sight, the riders—with their many-colored
dresses, their matchlocks with red flags, their jewelled
swords, their banners with long ribbons of all colors flying
in the wind—all galloping furiously, shouting, yelling, and
hissing, amidst a deafening din of thousands of horse-bells.

In order to accelerate our speed, a horseman rode by
my side lashing my pony to make it go its hardest.
Meanwhile the horseman who held the cord did his utmost to pull me out of the saddle, no doubt in the hope
of seeing me trampled to death by the cohort behind me.
As I leaned my body forward so as to maintain my seat,
and with my arms pulled violently backwards by the rope,
the flesh was rubbed off my hands and knuckles by the
chain of the handcuffs. In places the bone was exposed;
and, of course, every tug brought me into forcible contact
with the spikes and inflicted deeper wounds. The cord,
though strong, eventually and unexpectedly gave way.
The soldier who was pulling at the other end was clumsily unhorsed, and I myself was all but thrown by the unexpected jerk. This ludicrous incident at first provoked
mirth among my escort, a mirth which their superstitious
minds immediately turned into an ill omen.

THE RIDE ON A SPIKED SADDLE

When my pony was stopped, as well as the runaway steed of the dismounted cavalier, I took advantage of their fears, and assured them once more that whatever harm they tried to do me would go against themselves. However, the cord was retied with sundry strong knots, and, after an interruption of a few minutes, we resumed our breakneck gallop, I being again sent on in front.

Towards the end of our journey we had to go round the curve of a sand-hill, the track between this and a large

COAT I WORE AT THE TIME OF MY CAPTURE, AND SHOWING EFFECT OF SPIKES

pond at its foot being very narrow. At this point I saw in front of me a soldier posted in ambush, with his match-lock ready to fire. The pony sank deep in the sand, and could not travel fast here, which, I suppose, was the reason why this spot had been selected. The man fired as I passed only a few paces from him; but, as luck would have it, this second attempt also left me untouched.

Getting clear of the soft sand, and finding harder ground, we resumed our headlong career. Several arrows were shot at me from behind; but, though some passed very near, not one struck me; and thus, after an interminable ride, full of incident and excitement, we arrived, towards sunset, at our destination.

On the crown of a hill stood a fortress and large lamasery, and at its foot, in front of another large structure, the Pombo's gaudy tent had been pitched. The name of this place, as far as I could afterwards ascertain, was Namj Laccé Galshio or Gyatsho.

CHAPTER LXXXIV

Two or three men tore me roughly off the saddle.
The pain in my spine caused by the spikes was intense.
I asked for a moment's rest. My captors, however, refused, and, roughly thrusting me forward, said that I
would be beheaded in an instant. All the people round
jeered and made signs to me that my head would be cut
off, and insults of all kinds were showered upon me by
the crowd of Lamas and soldiers. I was hustled to the
execution-ground, which lay to the left front of the tent.
On the ground was a long log of wood in the shape of a
prism. Upon the sharp edge of this I was made to
stand, and several men held me by the body while four or
five others, using their combined strength, stretched my
legs as wide apart as they could go. Fixed in this painful position, the brutes securely tied me by my feet to the
log of wood with cords of yak-hair. Several men were
made to pull these cords, and they were so tight that
they cut grooves into my skin and flesh in several places
round my ankles and on my feet, many of the cuts* being
as much as three inches long.

When I was thus firmly bound, one ruffian, the man
Nerba, whom I have mentioned before as having fired a

---

* Measured some weeks later by Dr. Wilson.

shot at me, came forward and seized me from behind by
the hair of my head. My hair was long, as it had not
been cut for over five months.

The spectacle before me was overwhelming. By the
Pombo's tent stood in a row the most villanous brutes I
have ever set eyes upon. One, a powerful, repulsive individual, held in his hand a great knobbed mallet used for

A DISPLAY OF VARIOUS INSTRUMENTS OF TORTURE

fracturing bones; another carried a bow and arrows; a
third held a big two-handed sword; while others made a
display of various ghastly instruments of torture. The
crowd, thirsting for my blood, formed up in a semicircle,
leaving room for me to see the parade of torture implements that awaited me; and, as my eyes roamed from
one figure to the other, the several Lamas shook their
various implements to show that they were preparing for
action.

A group of three Lamas stood at the entrance of the
tent. They were the musicians. One held a gigantic

A BANNERMAN

horn which, when blown, emitted hoarse, thundering sounds, and his companions had one a drum and the other cymbals. Another fellow some distance away continually sounded a huge gong. From the moment I was made

LAMA MUSICIANS

to dismount the deafening sounds of this diabolical trio echoed all through the valley, and added to the horror of the scene.

An iron bar with a handle of wood bound in red cloth was being made red hot in a brasier. The Pombo, who had again placed something in his mouth to produce artificial foaming at the lips, and so to show his temper, worked himself up into a frenzy. A Lama handed him the implement of torture (the *Taram*), now red hot, and the Pombo seized it by the handle.

"*Ngaghi kiu meh taxon!*" (We will burn out your eyes!) cried a chorus of Lamas.

The Pombo strode up to me, brandishing the ghastly

implement. I stared at him, but he kept his eyes away from me. He seemed reluctant, but the Lamas around him urged him on, lifting the man's arm towards me!

"You have come to this country to see" (alluding to what I had stated the previous day—viz., that I was a traveller and pilgrim, and had only come to see the country). "This, then, is the punishment for you!" and with these dreadful words the Pombo raised his arm and placed the red-hot iron bar parallel to, and about an inch or two from, my eyeballs, and all but touching my nose.

Instinctively I kept my eyes tightly closed, but the heat was so intense that it seemed as if my eyes, the left one especially, were being desiccated and my nose scorched.

Though the time seemed interminable, I do not think that the heated bar was before my eyes actually longer than thirty seconds or so. Yet it was quite long enough, for, when I lifted my aching eyelids, I saw everything as in a red mist. My left eye was frightfully painful, and every few seconds it seemed as if something in front of it obscured its vision. With the right eye I could still see fairly well, except that everything, as I have said, looked red instead of its usual color. The hot iron had been thrown down and was frizzling on the wet ground a few paces from me.

THE TARAM

THE HOT IRON TORTURE.

CHAPTER LXXXV

My position as I stood with my legs wide apart, with
my back, hands, and legs bleeding, and seeing everything
of a ghastly red tinge; amidst the deafening, maddening
noise of gong, drum, cymbals, and horn; insulted, spat
upon by the crowd, and with Nerba holding me so tight
by my hair as to tear handfuls of it from my scalp, was
one in which I cannot wish even my bitterest enemies to
find themselves. All I was able to do was to remain calm
and composed and to watch with apparent unconcern the
preparations for the next sufferings to be inflicted upon
me.

" *Miumta nani sehko!*" (Kill him with a rifle!) shouted
a hoarse voice.

A matchlock was now being loaded by a soldier, and
such was the quantity of gunpowder they placed in the
barrel that I made sure whoever fired it would have his
head blown off; so it was with a certain amount of satisfaction that I saw it handed over to the Pombo. That
official placed the weapon against my forehead, with the
muzzle pointing upward. Then a soldier, leaning down,
applied fire to the fuse and eventually there was a loud report which gave my head a severe shock, and the over-
loaded matchlock flew clean out of the Pombo's hand,
much to everybody's surprise. I forced myself to laugh;

and their confusion, added to the tantalizing failure of every attempt they made to hurt me, drove the crowd to the highest pitch of fury.

"*Ta kossaton, ta kossaton!*" (Kill him, kill him!), exclaimed fierce voices all round me. "*Ngala mangbo shidak majidan!*" (We cannot frighten him!) "*Ta kossaton, ta kossaton!*" (Kill him, kill him!), the whole valley resounding with their ferocious cries.

A huge two-handed sword was now handed to the Pombo, who drew it out of its sheath.

"Kill him, kill him!" shouted the mob once more, urging on the executioner, who, his superstitious nature not having overcome the ill-omened fact that the matchlock a moment before had jumped out of his hand (which he probably attributed to the doing of some supreme power and not to the overcharge), seemed quite reluctant to come forward.

I seized this moment to say that they might kill me if they wished, but that, if I died to-day, they would all die to-morrow—an undeniable fact, for we are all bound to die some day. This seemed to cool them for a moment, but the excitement in the crowd was too great, and at last they succeeded in working the Pombo up into a passion. His face became quite unrecognizable, such was his excitement, and he behaved like a madman.

At this point a Lama approached and slipped something into the mouth of the executioner, who again foamed at the lips. A Lama held his sword, while he turned up one sleeve of his coat to have his arms free, and the Lamas turned up the other for him. Then he strode towards me with slow, ponderous steps, swinging the shiny, sharp blade from side to side before him, with his bare arms out-stretched.

The man Nerba, who was still holding me by the hair,

was told to make me bend my neck. I resisted with what little strength I had left, and, with the nervous courage of a doomed man, determined to keep my head erect and my forehead high. They might kill me, true enough, they might hack me to pieces if they chose, but never until I had lost my last atom of strength would these ruffians

THE EXECUTIONER BROUGHT THE SWORD DOWN TO MY NECK

make me stoop before them. I would perish, but it should be looking down upon the Pombo and his countrymen.

The executioner, now close to me, held the sword with his nervous hands, lifting it high above his shoulder. He then brought it down to my neck, which he touched with the blade, to measure the distance, as it were, for a clean effective stroke. Then, drawing back a step, he quickly raised the sword again and struck a blow at me with all his might. The sword passed disagreeably close to my neck, but did not touch me. I would not flinch, nor

speak, and my demeanor seemed to impress him almost
to the point of frightening him. He became reluctant to
continue his diabolical performance; but the impatience
and turbulence of the crowd were at their highest, and the
Lamas nearer to him gesticulated like madmen and urged
him on again.

As I write this, their wild shouts, their bloodthirsty
countenances, are vividly brought before me. Apparently
against his will, the executioner went through the same
kind of performance on the other side of my head. This
time the blade passed so near that the point cannot have
been more than half an inch or so from my neck.

It seemed as if all would soon be over; yet, strange to
say, even at this culminating moment I did not seriously
realize that I should die. Why this was so I cannot say,
because everything pointed towards my end being very
near; but I had a feeling all the time that I should live to
see the end of it all. I was very sorry, if my end were
really at hand, as it seemed likely, that I should die without seeing my parents and friends again, and that they
probably would never know how and where I had died.
One is naturally at all times reluctant to leave a world in
which one has barely had a dull moment, but, after all my
wretched experiences, sufferings, and excitement, I did not
realize my peril so much as I should have done had I, for
instance, been dragged from my comfortable London flat
direct onto the execution-ground, instead of first having
lived through the recent past.

Naturally the scene is one that I am not likely to forget, and I must say for the Tibetans that the whole affair
was very picturesquely carried out. Even the ghastliest
ceremonies may have their artistic side, and this particular
one, performed with extra pomp and flourish, was really
impressive.

It appears that the unpleasant sword exercise is sometimes gone through in Tibet previous to actually cutting off the head, so as to make the victim suffer more before the final blow is given. I was not aware of this at the time, and only learned it some weeks after. It is usually at the third stroke that the victim is actually beheaded.

The Lamas were still clamoring for my head, but the Pombo made a firm stand this time, and declined to go on with the execution. They collected round him and seemed very angry; they shouted and yelled and gesticulated in the wildest fashion ; and still the Pombo kept his eyes upon me in a half-respectful, half-frightened manner, and refused to move.

CHAPTER LXXXVI

An excited consultation followed, during which, in the midst of this scene of barbarity, my coolie Mansing arrived. He had fallen off his bare-back pony many times, and had been left far behind. The man who held my hair now relinquished his grasp, while another pushed me violently from in front, causing me to fall heavily backward, and putting a painful strain on all the tendons of my legs. Mansing, bruised and aching all over, was brought forward and tied by his legs to the same log of wood to which I was fastened. They informed me that they would kill my coolie first, and one brutal Lama seized him roughly by the throat. I was pushed up in a sitting posture, and a cloth was thrown over my head and face, so that I could not see what was being done. I heard poor Mansing groan pitifully, then there was a dead silence. I called him, I received no answer; so I concluded that he had been despatched. I was left in this terrible suspense for over a quarter of an hour, when at last they removed the cloth from over my head, and I beheld my coolie lying before me, bound to the log and almost unconscious, but, thank God, still alive. He told me that, when I had called him, a Lama had placed his hand upon his mouth to prevent him from answering, while, with the other hand, he had squeezed his neck so tightly as to nearly strangle him. After a while Mansing

146

got better, and the coolness and bravery of the poor
wretch during these terrible trials were really marvellous.

We were told that our execution was only postponed
till the next day, in order that we might be tortured until
the time came for us to be brought out to death.

A number of Lamas and soldiers stood round jeering
at us. I seized the opportunity this respite afforded to
hail a swaggering Lama and ask him for some refresh-
ment.

"*Orehch, orehch nga dappa lugn duh, chuen deh, dang,
yak, guram, tcha, tsamba pin!*" (I am very hungry, please
give me some rice, yak meat, *ghur*, tea, and oatmeal!) I
asked in my best Tibetan.

"*Hum murr, Maharaja!*" (I want butter, your Majesty!)
put in Mansing, half in Hindustani and half in the Tibetan language.

This natural application for food seemed to afford intense amusement to our torturers, who had formed a ring
round us, and laughed at our appeal, while Mansing and
I, both of us famished, were left sitting bound in a most
painful position.

The day had now waned, and our torturers did not fail
to constantly remind us that the following day our heads
would be severed from our bodies, which I told them
would cause us no pain, for if they gave us no food we
should be dead of starvation by then.

Whether they realized that this might be the case, or
whether some other reasons moved them, I cannot say;
but several of the Lamas, who had been most brutal, in-
cluding one who had the previous day taken a part in
Chanden Sing's flogging, now became quite polite and
treated us with a surprising amount of deference. Two
Lamas were despatched to the monastery, and returned
after some time with bags of *tsamba* and a large *raksang*

of boiling tea. I have hardly ever enjoyed a meal more, though the Lamas stuffed the food down my throat with their unwashed fingers so fast that they nearly choked me.

"Eat, eat as much as you can," said they, grimly, "for it may be your last meal."

And eat I did, and washed the *tsamba* down with quantities of buttered tea, which they poured into my mouth carelessly out of the *raksang*.

Mansing, whose religion did not allow him to eat food touched by folk of a different caste, was eventually permitted to lick the meal out of the wooden bowl. I myself was none too proud to take the food in any way it might be offered, and when my humble, "*Orcheh, orcheh tchuen mangbo tcrokchi*," (Please give me some more) met with the disapproval of the Lamas, and brought out the everlasting negative, "*Middū, middū*," I was still too hungry to waste any of the precious food: so the Tibetans revolved the wooden bowl round and round my mouth, and I licked it as clean as if it had never been used.

CHAPTER LXXXVII

HAPPINESS CHECKED—STRETCHED ON THE RACK—MANSING SHARES MY
FATE—DRENCHED AND IN RAGS—AN UNSOLVED MYSTERY

AFTER all the excitement of the day, we were beginning
to feel a little restored and much relieved at being treated
rather less roughly, were it only for a few moments, when,
small as it was, the improvement in our condition was
checked.

A Lama came from the monastery and gave orders
right and left, and the place was again in commotion.
We were pounced upon and roughly seized, and my legs
were quickly untied, a number of men holding me down
the while. Again they lifted me until I stood upright on
the cutting edge of the prismatic log: two men seized
one leg and two the other, and stretched them apart as
far as they could possibly go. Then rope after rope was
wound round my feet and ankles, and I was made fast as
before to the log.

As my legs were much farther apart this time, the pain
in the muscles of my legs when they proceeded to knock
me down backward was even greater than it had been on
the previous occasion. But before I had time to feel it
in full, the Lamas, now as ferocious as I had seen them at
first, dragged my manacled arms backward from under
my body and tied a rope to the chain of the handcuffs.
This done, they passed the rope through a hole in the
top of a high post behind me, and by tugging at it,
strained my arms upward in a way that, had I been less

supple, would certainly have broken them. When all their strength combined could not stretch me another inch without tearing my body to pieces, they made the rope fast, and I remained half suspended, and feeling as if all the bones of my limbs were getting, or had got, pulled out of their sockets. The weight of the body naturally tending to settle down would, I felt, every moment increase the suffering of this terrible torture, which was really a primitive form of the rack.

Mansing was likewise suspended on the other side, his feet remaining tied to the log to which my own were fastened, only not quite so wide apart.

The pain was at first intense, the tendons of the legs and arms being dreadfully strained, and the spinal column bent so as nearly to be broken in two. The shoulder-blades, forced into close contact, pressed the vertebræ inward, and caused excruciating pains along the lumbar vertebræ, where the strain was greatest.

As if this were not sufficient, a cord was tied from Mansing's neck to mine, the object of which was to keep our necks stretched in a most uncomfortable position.

It began to rain heavily, and we were left out in the open. The rags to which our clothes had been reduced in our struggle when we were first seized were drenched. Half naked and wounded, we were alternately numbed with cold and burning with fever. A guard encircled us, having with them two watch-dogs tied to pegs. The soldiers were apparently so confident of our inability to escape that they drew their heavy blankets over their heads and slept. One of them in his slumber moved and pushed his sword outside the blanket in which he had now rolled himself tight. This inspired me with the idea of attempting to escape.

Two or three hours later it had become very dark.

Thanks to the extremely supple nature of my hands, I succeeded in drawing the right hand out of my handcuffs, and, after an hour or so of stealthy and anxious work I managed to unloose the cord that bound Mansing's feet. Then I whispered to him to get up slowly and to push the sword towards me with his foot until I could reach it.

THUS ELAPSED TWENTY-FOUR TERRIBLE HOURS

If successful in this, I could soon cut my bonds and those fastening Mansing's hands, and with a weapon in our possession we would make a bold dash for liberty.

Mansing, however, was not a champion of agility. In his joy at feeling partly free, the poor coolie moved his stiff legs clumsily. The vigilant watch-dogs detected this, and gave the alarm by barking. The guards were up in a moment, and, timid as they always were, they all hurriedly left us, and went to fetch lights to examine our bonds.

In the meanwhile, protected by the darkness of the

stormy night, I had succeeded in replacing my hand inside the iron handcuff. Putting it back was more difficult than drawing it out, but I had just time to effect my purpose. The men who had gone to the monastery returned with lights. I pretended to be fast asleep: a likely thing with every bone in my body feeling as if it were disjointed, every limb numbed and frozen, every tendon and ligament so strained as to drive me mad with pain!

The Tibetans found the bonds round Mansing's feet undone. They examined my hands and saw them just as they had left them. They inspected my feet. The ropes were still there, cutting into my flesh. They inspected Mansing's hands, only to find them still fastened to the post behind him.

The Tibetans were so puzzled at this mysterious occurrence that they positively got frightened. They began to shout excitedly, calling for help. In a moment, the alarm having been given, a crowd of men rushed at us, and, with their swords drawn, surrounded us. One man, braver than the rest, gave Mansing a few cuts with a whip, warning us that if the ropes were found undone again they would decapitate us there and then. The coolie was again bound, this time more tightly than ever.

By way of precaution, a light was set between Mansing and myself, and, as it was still raining hard, the Tibetans placed a canvas shelter over us to prevent the light from being extinguished. At about six or seven in the morning Mansing's feet were untied, but not his hands. I was left in the same uncomfortable and painful posture. The hours passed very slowly and wearily. My legs, my arms, and hands had gradually become quite lifeless, and after the first six or seven hours that I had been stretched on the rack, I felt no more actual pain. The numbness crept along every limb of my body, until I had now the peculiar sensation of possessing a living head on a dead body.

It is indeed remarkable how one's brain keeps alive and working well under such circumstances, apparently unaffected by the temporary mortification of the remainder of the system.

The day now dawning was one full of strange incidents. When the sun was high in the sky, the Pombo, with a great number of Lamas, rode down from the monastery, though the distance was very short. He went to his tent, and presently my cases of scientific instruments were brought outside and opened, the soldiers and Lamas displaying an amusing mixture of curiosity and caution over everything they touched. I had to explain the use of each instrument, a difficult matter indeed, considering their ignorance and my limited knowledge of Tibetan, which did not allow of my delivering scientific addresses. The sextant was looked upon with great suspicion, and even more so the hypsometrical apparatus, with its thermometers in brass tubes, which they took to be some sort of firearm. Then came a lot of undeveloped photographic plates, box after box of which they opened in broad daylight, destroying in a few moments all the valuable negatives that I had taken since leaving Mansarowar. The Pombo, more observant than the others, noticed that the plates turned a yellowish color on being exposed to the light.

" Why is that ?" asked he.

" It is a sign that you will suffer for what you are doing to me."

The Pombo flung away the plate, and was much upset. He ordered a hole to be dug in the ground some way off, and the plates to be instantly buried. The soldiers, however, who had been intrusted with the order, seemed loth to touch the plates, and they had to be reprimanded and beaten by the Lamas before they would obey. At last, with their feet, they shoved the boxes of negatives to a spot some distance off, where, in dog fashion, they dug a deep hole with their hands in the muddy ground; and there, alas ! I saw my work of several weeks covered forever with earth.

Now came my paint-box with its cakes of water-colors.

" What do you do with these ?" cried an angry Lama, pointing at the harmless colors.

" I paint pictures."

" No, you are lying. With the ' yellow ' you find where

gold is in the country, and with the 'blue' you discover where malachite is."

I assured them that this was not the case, and told them that if they would untie me I would, on recovering the use of my arms, paint a picture before them.

They prudently preferred to leave me tied up.

Their whole attention was now drawn to a considerable sum in silver and gold which they found in the cases, and the Pombo warned the people that not one coin must be stolen.

I took this chance to make an offering of 500 rupees to the Lamasery, and told the Pombo that I would like him to accept as a gift my Martini-Henry, which I had noticed rather took his fancy.

Both gifts were refused, as they said the Lamasery was very wealthy and the Pombo's position as an official did not allow him to carry a rifle. The Pombo, nevertheless, was quite touched by the offer, and came personally to thank me.

In a way the rascals were gentlemanly enough in their manner, and I could not help admiring their mixture of courtesy and cruelty, either of which they could switch on at a moment's notice without regard to the other.

CHAPTER LXXXIX

THEY had now reached the bottom of the water-tight
case, and the Pombo drew out with much suspicion a
curious flattened object.

"What is that?" inquired he, as usual lifting the article
up in the air.

My sight had been so injured that I could not clearly
discern what it was; but on their waving it in front of my
nose, I recognized it to be my long mislaid bath-sponge,
dry and flattened, which Chanden Sing, with his usual
ability for packing, had stored away at the bottom of the
case, piling upon it the heavy cases of photographic plates.
The sponge, a very large one, was now reduced to the
thickness of less than an inch, owing to the weight that
had for weeks lain upon it.

The Tibetans were greatly puzzled at this new discovery, which they said resembled tinder; and it was touched
with much caution, for some of the Lamas said it might
explode.

When their curiosity was appeased, they took it and
threw it away. It fell near me in a small pool of water.
This was a golden opportunity to frighten my jailers, and
I addressed the sponge in English, and with any word
that came into my mouth, pretending to utter incantations. The attention of the Lamas and soldiers was naturally quickly drawn to this unusual behavior on my part;

and they could not conceal their terror when, as I spoke louder and louder to the sponge, it gradually swelled to its normal size with the moisture it absorbed.

The Tibetans, who at first could hardly believe their eyes at this incomprehensible occurrence, became so panic-stricken at what they believed to be an exhibition of my occult powers, that there was a general stampede in every direction.

In a way, all this was entertaining, and anyhow it

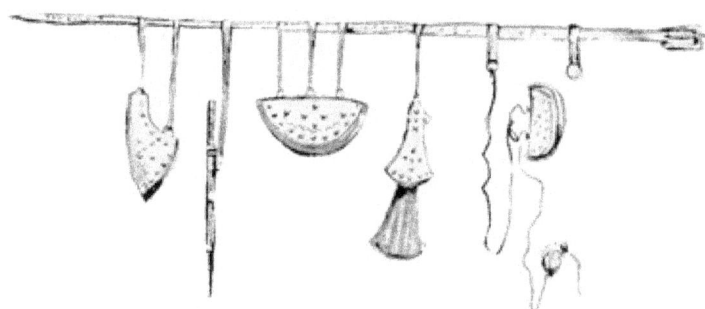

BELT, WITH BULLET AND POWDER POUCHES, DAGGER, NEEDLE-CASE, AND FLINT AND STEEL

served to pass away the time. The most amusing scene that afternoon was, however, still to come.

After a time the Lamas screwed up their courage, and returned to where my baggage had been overhauled. One of them picked up my Martini-Henry, and the others urged him to fire it off. He came to me, and when I had explained to him how to load it, he took a cartridge and placed it in the breech, but would insist on not closing the bolt firmly home. When I warned him of the consequences, he struck me over the head with the butt of the rifle.

It is the fashion, when aiming with one of their match-locks, which have a prop attached to them, to place the butt in front of the nose instead of holding it firmly to the shoulder as we do. So the Lama aimed in this fashion at one of my yaks peacefully grazing some thirty yards off. While everybody watched anxiously to see the results of this marksman's shooting, he pulled the trigger; the rifle went off with an extra loud report, and behold! the muzzle of the Martini burst and the violent recoil gave the Lama a fearful blow in the face. The rifle, flying out of his hands, described a somersault in the air, and the

MARTINI-HENRY EXPLODED

Lama fell backward to the ground, where he remained spread out flat, bleeding all over and screaming like a child. His nose was squashed, one eye had been put out, and his teeth shattered.

Whether the rifle burst because the bolt had not been properly closed, or because mud had got into the muzzle as well, I could not say; but I give here a photograph of the broken weapon, which the Tibetans returned to me several months later through the Government of India.

The injured Lama, I may say, was the one at the head of the party that wanted to have my head cut off, so that, naturally enough, I could not help betraying my satisfaction at the accident. I was glad they had let me live another day, were it only to see his self-inflicted punishment.

158

THE Pombo, who had been, during the greater part of
the afternoon, looking at me with an air of mingled pity
and respect, as though he had been forced against his
will to treat me so brutally, could not help joining in
my laughter at the Lama's sorrowful plight. In a way,
I believe he was rather glad that the accident had happened; for, if he had until then been uncertain whether
to kill me or not, he felt, after what had occurred, that
it was not prudent to attempt it. The gold ring which
had been taken from me on the day of our arrest, and
for which I had asked many times, as it had been given
by my mother, was regarded as possessing miraculous
powers as long as it was upon me; and was therefore
kept well away from me, for fear that, with its help, I
might break my bonds and escape. The Pombo, the
Lamas and officers held another consultation, at the end
of which, towards sunset, several soldiers came and
loosed my legs from the stretching log; and my hands,
though still manacled, were lowered from the pillar
behind.

As the ropes round my ankles were unwound from
the deep channels they had cut into my flesh, large
patches of skin came away with them. Thus ended the
most terrible twenty-four hours I have ever passed in
my lifetime.

I felt very little relief at first as I lay flat on the ground, for my body and legs were stiff and as if dead; and as time went by and I saw no signs of their coming back to life, I feared that mortification had set in, and that I had lost the use of my feet for good. It was two or three hours before the blood began to circulate in my right foot, and the pain when it did so was intense. Had a handful of knives been passed slowly down the inside of my leg the agony could not have been more excruciating. My arms were not quite so bad; they also were numbed, but the circulation was more quickly re-established.

In the meanwhile the Pombo, whether to amuse me or to show off his riches, ordered about one hundred ponies, some with magnificent harness, to be brought up; and mounting the finest, and holding in his hand that dreadful *taram*, rode round the hill on which the monastery and fort stood.

On returning, he harangued his men and a series of sports began, the Pombo seating himself near me and watching me intently to see how I was enjoying the performance. First of all the best marksmen were selected, and with their matchlocks fired one after the other at my two poor yaks, only a few yards off; but although they aimed carefully and deliberately, they did not succeed in hitting them. I knew that they fired with bullets, for I could hear the hissing sound the missiles made.

Next came a display of fine horsemanship, which was very interesting. I should have enjoyed it more if I had not been suffering agonies all the time. Still, the performance helped to cheer me. First there were races in which only two ponies at a time took part, the last race being run between the two winners of the last heats, and a *kata* was presented to the victor. Next one horseman rode ahead at full gallop flying a *kata*, while some twenty others followed closely behind. The *kata* was left to fly by itself, and when it settled on the ground, the horsemen following the first rode some distance away, and, at a given signal, galloped back wildly, all converging towards the spot, and, bending down from their ponies, attempted to pick up the *kata* without dismounting. Some of the younger men were very clever at this.

Another exercise consisted in one man on foot standing still, while a mounted comrade rode at full gallop towards him, seized him by his clothes, and lifted him on to the saddle.

Though I could not see as well as I wished, I got so interested in the show, and expressed such admiration for the ponies, that the Pombo, becoming quite thoughtful and polite, ordered the best of them to be brought before me, and had me lifted into a sitting posture, so that I could see them better.

THIS was a great relief, for I was suffering more from my humiliating position, being unable to stand, than from the tortures themselves. The Pombo told me that I must now look towards the tent, and then got up and walked towards it.

The opening of the tent was over twenty feet long. Some soldiers came and dragged me close to the front of it, so that I could witness all that went on.

Two big Lamas entered the tent with the Pombo, and a number of other people who were inside were turned out. They closed the tent for a few minutes, and then opened it again. In the mean time a gong summoned the Lamas of the monastery to come down, and, a few minutes later, a string of them came and took their places inside the tent.

The Pombo, in his yellow coat and trousers and four-cornered hat, sat on a kind of high-backed chair in the centre of the tent, and by his side stood the two Lamas who had first entered it with him. The Pombo was beyond doubt in a hypnotic trance. He sat motionless, with his hands flat on his knees and his head erect; his eyes were fixed and staring. For some minutes he remained like this, and all the soldiers and people who had collected in front of the tent went down on their knees, laid their caps on the ground, and muttered prayers. One of

the two Lamas, a fellow with great mesmeric powers, now
laid his hand upon the shoulders of the Pombo, who
gradually raised his arms with hands out-stretched and
remained as in a cataleptic state for a long time without
moving an inch.

Next the Lama touched the Pombo's neck with his
thumbs, and caused the head to begin a rapid circular
movement from left to right.

THE POMBO'S CONTORTIONS

Certain exorcisms were pronounced by the hypnotizer,
and the Pombo now began the most extraordinary snake-
like contortions, moving and twisting his arms, head,
body, and legs. He worked himself, or rather was worked,
into a frenzy that lasted some time, and the crowd of
devotees drew nearer and nearer to him, praying fervently and emitting deep sighs and cries of astonishment and
almost terror at some of the more eccentric movements

of his limbs. Every now and then this weird kind of dance terminated in a strange posture, the Pombo actually doubling himself up with his head between his feet and his long flat hat resting on the ground. While he was in this position, the bystanders went one by one to finger his feet and make low prostrations and salaams. At last the hypnotizer, seizing the Pombo's head between his hands,

THE FINALE OF THE DANCE

stared in his eyes, rubbed his forehead, and woke him from the trance. The Pombo was pale and exhausted. He lay back on the chair and his hat fell off his head, which was clean shaven, thus unmistakably showing that he, too, was a Lama, and, as we have seen, of a very high order, probably of the first rank after the Dalai Lama.

Katas were distributed after this religious performance to all the Tibetans present, and they folded them and stowed them away in their coats.

THE Pombo came out of his gaudy tent, and I told him
that the dance was beautiful, but that I was very hungry.
He asked me what I wanted to eat, and I said I would
like some meat and tea.

A little later, a large vessel with a delicious stew of
yak's meat was brought to me, as well as *tsamba* in abundance. However, though I felt quite famished, I had the
greatest difficulty in swallowing even a little food. This
I thought must be owing to the injuries to my spine and
to the mortification of my limbs, which had apparently
affected my whole system.

When the Pombo had retired and night came on, I
was again tied to the stretching log, but this time with
my limbs not stretched so far apart. My hands, too,
were again fastened to the pillar behind, but with no
strain on them.

Late in the evening half a dozen Lamas came from
the monastery with a light and a large brass bowl which
they said contained tea. The wounded Lama, with his
head all bandaged up, was among them, and he was so
anxious for me to drink some of it to keep myself warm
during the cold night that I became quite suspicious.
When they pushed a bowl of it to my lips I merely
sipped a little, and declined to take more, spitting out

what they had forced into my mouth. I swallowed a few drops, and a few minutes later I was seized with sharp, excruciating pains in my stomach, which continued for several days after. I can but conclude that the drink proffered me was poisoned.

The following day my left foot, which had remained lifeless since I had been untied from the rack the first time, began to get better, and the circulation was gradually restored. The pain was unbearable.

In the morning indecision again prevailed as to what was to be done to us. A number of Lamas were still anxious to have us beheaded, whereas the Pombo and the others had the previous night almost made up their minds to send us back to the frontier. Unfortunately, it appears* that the Pombo had seen a vision during the night in which a spirit told him that, if he did not kill us, he and his country would suffer some great misfortune. " You can kill the Plenki," the spirit was reported to have said, " and no one will punish you if you do. The Plenkis are afraid to fight the Tibetans."

Among the Lamas no important step is taken without incantations and reference to occult science, so the Pombo ordered a Lama to cut off a lock of my hair, which he did with a very blunt knife, and then the Pombo rode up with it in his hand to the Lamasery to consult the oracle. The lock was handed in for inspection, and it seems that, after certain incantations, the oracle answered that I must be beheaded or the country would be in great danger.

The Pombo rode back apparently disappointed, and now ordered that one of my toe-nails should be cut ; after which operation, performed with the same blunt knife,

---

* The Tibetan Lamas stated this to the Political Peshkar Karak Sing, our frontier officer.

the oracle was again consulted as to what should be done, and unhappily gave the same answer.

Three such consultations are usually held by the high court of the assembled Lamas, the Tibetans on the third occasion producing for the oracle's decision a piece of a finger-nail. The Lama who was about to cut this off examined my hands behind and spread my fingers apart, expressing great surprise and astonishment. In a moment all the Lamas and soldiers came round and examined my manacled hands—a repetition of my experience at the Tucker Monastery. The Pombo, too, on being informed, immediately came and inspected my fingers, and the proceedings were at once stopped.

When some weeks later I was released, I was able to learn from the Tibetans the reason of their amazement. My fingers happen to be webbed rather higher than usual, and this is most highly thought of in Tibet. He who possesses such fingers has, according to the Tibetans, a charmed life, and, no matter how much one tries, no harm can be done to him. Aside from the question whether there was much charm or not in my life in Tibet, there is no doubt that this trifling superstition did much towards hastening the Pombo's decision as to what was to be our fate.

CHAPTER XCIII

OUR LIVES TO BE SPARED—AN UNPLEASANT MARCH—CHANDEN SING
STILL ALIVE—A SLEEPLESS NIGHT—TOWARDS THE FRONTIER—LONG
AND PAINFUL MARCHES—HOW WE SLEPT AT NIGHT—A MAP DRAWN
WITH BLOOD

THE Pombo ordered that my life should be spared, and that I should on that very day start on my return journey towards the Indian frontier. He took from my own money one hundred and twenty rupees, which he placed in my pocket for my wants during the journey, and commanded that, though I must be kept chained up, I was to be treated kindly, and my servants also.

When all was ready, Mansing and I were led on foot to Toxem, our guard consisting of some fifty horsemen riding on ponies. We had to travel at a great speed despite our severely lacerated feet, our aching bones, and the sores and wounds with which we were covered all over. The soldiers led me tied by the neck like a dog, and dragged me along when, panting, exhausted, and suffering, I could not keep up with the ponies. We crossed several cold streams, sinking in water and mud up to our waists.

At Toxem, to my great delight, I beheld Chanden Sing still alive. He had been kept prisoner in the mud-house, where he had remained tied upright to a post for over three days, and for four days he had not eaten food nor drank anything. He was told that I had been beheaded. He was in a dreadful condition, almost dying from his wounds, cold, and starvation.

CHANDEN SING TIED TO A POST

We were detained there for the night, half-choked by smoke in one of the rooms of the mud-house packed with soldiers, who, with a woman of easy morals, gambled the whole night, and sang and swore and fought, preventing us from sleeping for even a few minutes.

The next day at sunrise Chanden Sing and I were placed

A WHITE YAK

on yaks, not on riding saddles, but on pack-saddles such as those shown in the illustration in Chapter XL of Vol. I. Poor Mansing was made to walk, and was beaten mercilessly when, tired and worn out, he fell or remained behind. They again tied him with a rope by the neck and dragged him along in a most brutal manner. We had a strong guard to prevent our escaping, and they demanded fresh relays of yaks and ponies and food for themselves at all the encampments, so that we travelled very fast. In the first five days we covered one hundred and seventy-eight miles, the two longest marches being respectively forty-two and forty-five miles; but afterwards we did not cover quite such great distances.

We suffered considerably on these long marches, as the soldiers ill-treated us and would not allow us to eat every day for fear we should get too strong. They let us have food only every two or three days, and our exhaustion and the pain caused by riding those wretched yaks in our wounded condition were terrible.

All our property had been taken away from us, and our clothes were in rags and swarming with vermin. We were barefooted and practically naked. The first few days we generally marched from before sunrise till sometimes an hour or two after sunset; and when we reached camp we were torn off our yaks and our jailers fastened iron cuffs round our ankles, in addition to those we had already round our wrists. Being considered quite safe, we were left to sleep out in the open without a covering of any kind, and often lying on snow or deluged with rain. Our guard generally pitched a tent under which they slept; but even when they did not have one, they usually went to brew their tea some fifty yards or so from us.

Helped by my two servants, who sat by me to keep watch and to screen me, I managed, at considerable risk, to keep a rough record of the journey back, on a small piece of paper that had remained in my pocket when I had been searched by the Tibetans. As I did when on the rack, I used to draw my right hand out of its cuff, and, with a small piece of bone I had picked up as pen, and my blood as ink, I drew brief cipher notes, and a map of the whole route back.

Necessarily, as I had no instruments with which to take careful observations. I had to content myself with taking

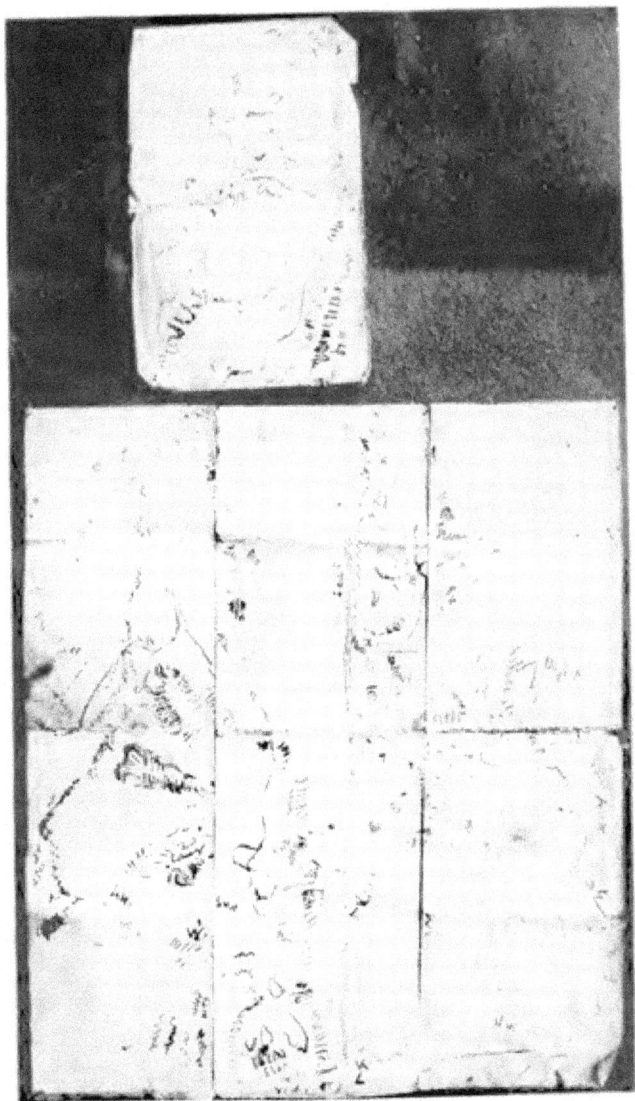

MAP DRAWN IN BLOOD DURING CAPTIVITY

my bearings by the sun, the position of which I got fairly accurately by constantly watching the shadow projected by my body on the ground. Of course, when it rained or snowed I was altogether at a loss, and had to reckon my bearings by the observations of the previous day.

CHAPTER XCIV

SOUTH OF THE OUTWARD JOURNEY—SEVERITY OF OUR GUARD—VEN-
TRILOQUISM AND ITS EFFECTS—TERRIBLE BUT INSTRUCTIVE DAYS
— THE SOUTHERN SOURCE OF THE BRAHMAPUTRA—LEAVING YUT-
ZANG

WE travelled, as can be seen in the dotted red line on
the map attached to this book, first west, then west-northwest, northwest, west, and northwest, following the Brahmaputra along a course south of the outward journey, until we reached the boundary of the Yutzang* (central, or
Lhassa) province. Our guard were not only severe with
us, but they also ill-treated us in every possible way. One
or two of the soldiers, however, showed kindness and
thoughtfulness, bringing us a little butter or *tsamba* whenever they could do so unseen by their comrades. The
guard was changed so frequently that we had no chance
of making friends with them, and each lot seemed worse
than the last.

A very curious incident happened one day, causing a
scare among them. We had halted near a cliff, and the
soldiers were some twenty yards off. Having exhausted
every means I could think of to inspire these ruffians with
respect, I resorted to the performance of some ventrilo-
quial feats, pretending to speak and to receive the an-
swers from the summit of the cliff. The Tibetans were
terror-stricken. They asked me who was up there. I
said it was some one I knew.

" Is it a Plenki?"

" Yes."

Immediately they hustled us on our yaks, and mounting their ponies, we left the place at headlong speed.

On reaching a spot which from observations taken on my outward journey I reckoned to be in longitude 83° 6'

ONE OF OUR GUARD

30" east and latitude 30° 27' 30" north I had a great piece of luck. It is at this point that the two principal sources of the Brahmaputra meet and form one river, the one coming from the northwest, which I had already followed, the other proceeding from the west-northwest. The Tibetans, to my delight, selected the southern route, thus giving me the opportunity of visiting the second of the two principal sources of the great river. This second stream rises in a flat plain, having its first birth in a lakelet in approximate longitude 82° 47′ east and latitude 30° 33′ north. I gave the northern source my own name, a proceeding which I trust will not be regarded as immodest in view of the fact that I was the first European to visit it, and of all the circumstances of my journey.

This period of our captivity was dreary, yet interesting and instructive, for, as we went along, I got the soldiers to teach me some Tibetan songs, not unlike those of the Shokas in character, and from the less ill-natured men of our guard I picked up, by judicious questioning, a considerable amount of information, which, together with that collected from my own observations, I have given in this book.

Over a more southerly and lower pass than the Maium Pass, by which, healthy, hopeful and free, we had entered the province of Yutzang, we now left it, wounded, broken down, naked and prisoners.

EASTER TIMES — LARGE ENCAMPMENTS — SUFFOCATING A GOAT — A TARJUM'S ENCAMPMENT — TOKCHIM—OLD FRIENDS — MUSICIANS — CHARITY

WE now proceeded in a northwesterly direction, and, once clear of the sacred Yutzang province, our guard behaved with rather less cruelty. With the little money the Pombo had permitted me to keep we were allowed to purchase food enough to provide us with more frequent meals, and, while we ate, the soldiers removed our handcuffs, which they temporarily placed round our ankles. Thus, with utensils lent us by our guard, we were able to cook some food; and, although we had to serve it on flat stones instead of dishes, it seemed indeed delicious.

We crossed over our former track, and then followed it almost in a parallel line, but some miles north of it, along an undulating, clayey plateau, thus avoiding the marshy plain which we had found so troublesome to cross on our journey out. We found large numbers of black tents here and there, and one night, when we were encamped by some small lakes, we were permitted to purchase a goat. A soldier, a good fellow who had been very friendly to us, selected a fine fat one for us, and we were looking forward with pleasure to a solid meal, when we found to our dismay that we had no means of despatching the animal. We could not behead it, as the Tibetans would not trust us with a knife or sword, and the Tibetans themselves refused to kill the animal for us in any other way. Event-

ually our soldier friend allowed his scruples to be overcome by the payment of a rupee, and proceeded to kill
the animal in a most cruel fashion. He tied its legs together, and, having stuffed the nostrils with mud, he held
the poor beast's mouth closed with one hand until it was
suffocated. The soldier during the performance revolved
his prayer-wheel with his free hand, praying fervently all
the while.

We found ourselves at last in the plain, where a Tarjum's encampment of some two hundred tents was to be

SOLDIER SUFFOCATING GOAT

seen, and here we remained one night. There was a large
assemblage of Lamas and soldiers. In the middle of the
night we were suddenly and roughly roused from sleep,
and made to move our camp about a mile or so from the
settlement; and, early in the morning, having crossed the
large stream, we proceeded in a southwestly direction,

STROLLING MUSICIANS

reaching the encampment of the Tokchim Tarjum the same night. Here we were met by the officers who had on a previous occasion brought us gifts, and whom we had routed with all their soldiers when they threatened us.

This time they behaved very decently, the oldest of them showing us every civility, and professing great admiration for our courage in persevering against such heavy odds. The old gentleman did all he could to make us comfortable, and even called up two strolling musicians for our amusement. One man wore a peculiar four-cornered headdress made of skin. He played with a bow on a two-stringed instrument, while his companion, a child, danced and went through certain clumsy contortions, going round every few minutes with his tongue thrust out to beg for *tsamba* from the audience. The Tibetans are very charitable towards beggars, and not only on this, but on other occasions, I noticed that they seldom re-

OLD BEGGAR

fused, no matter however small their donations might be, to give *tsamba* or pieces of butter or *chura* to the mendicants. The older musician had a square club passed through his girdle, and at intervals he laid down his instrument, and, using the club as a sword, gave an imita-

177

tion of a martial dance, exactly like the one I have described as performed by the Shokas. Every now and then, too, he applied it to the boy's back and head, to inspire him with fresh vigor, and this generally drew roars of laughter from the audience.

THE next day, amid repeated good-byes and professions of friendship on the part of our hosts and jailers, we departed towards Mansarowar, and late in the afternoon reached the Tucker village and Gomba, where we put up at the same *serai* in which I had slept on my way out. All our bonds were here removed for good, and we enjoyed comparative freedom, though four men walked by my side wherever I went, and an equal number looked after Chanden Sing and Mansing. Naturally we were not allowed to go far from the *serai*, but we could prowl about in the village. I took this opportunity to have a swim in the Mansarowar Lake, and Chanden Sing and Mansing again paid fresh salaams to the gods and plunged in the sacred water.

The Lamas, who had been so friendly during my former visit, were now extremely sulky and rude; and, after having witnessed our arrival, they all withdrew into the monastery, banging the gate after them. All the villagers, too, hastily retired to their respective houses. The place was deserted with the exception of the soldiers round us.

Poor Mansing, who, worn out and in great pain, was sitting close by me, looking vaguely at the lake, had an extraordinary vision, the result, probably, of fever or exhaustion.

"Oh, sahib," said he, as if in a dream, though he was quite awake; "look, look! Look at the crowd of people walking on the water. There must be more than a thousand men! Oh, how big they are getting! . . . And there is God! . . . Seva. . . . No; they are Tibetans; they are coming to kill us; they are Lamas! Oh, come, sahib, they are so near! . . . Oh, they are flying. . . ."

"Where are they?" I asked.

I could see that the poor fellow was under an hallucination. His forehead was burning, and he was in a high fever.

"They have all disappeared!" he exclaimed, as I placed my hand on his forehead and he woke from his trance.

He seemed quite stupefied for a few moments; and, on my inquiring of him later whether he had seen the phantom crowd again, he could not remember ever having seen it at all.

A TIBETAN SHEPHERD

The natives came to visit us in the *serai* during the evening, and we had great fun with them, for the Tibetans are full of humor and have many comical ways. As for ourselves, now that we were only two marches from Taklakot, it was but natural that our spirits were high. Only two more days of captivity, and then a prospect of freedom.

It was still dark when we were roused and ordered to start. The soldiers dragged us out of the *serai*. We entreated them to let us have another plunge in the sacred Mansarowar, and the three of us were eventually allowed

INTERIOR OF A SERAI

to do so. The water was bitterly cold, and we had nothing to dry ourselves with.

It was about an hour before sunrise when we were placed on our yaks and, surrounded by some thirty soldiers, rode off.

WHEN we had been marching for several hours, our guard halted to have their tea. A man named Suna, and his brother and son, whom I had met in Garbyang, halted near us, and from them I heard that news had arrived in India that I and my two men had been beheaded, and that there-upon Doctor Wilson and the Political Peshkar Karak Sing had crossed over the frontier to ascertain the facts, and to attempt to recover my baggage, etc. My joy was intense when I heard that they were still at Taklakot. I persuaded Su-na to return as fast as he could, and in-form Wilson that I was a prisoner, and tell

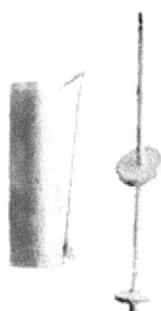

TEA CHURN (OPEN)

him my whereabouts. I had barely given Suna this mes-sage when our guard seized the man and his brother and roughly dismissed them, preventing them from having any further communication with us. As soon as we were on the march again, a horseman rode up to us with strict orders from the Jong Pen of Taklakot not to let us pro-ceed any farther towards the frontier by the Lippu Pass, which we could now have reached in two days, but to take us round by the distant Lumpiya Pass. At this

time of the year the Lumpiya would be impassable, and
we should have to make a further journey of at least fifteen or sixteen days, most of it over snow and ice, during
which we, in our starved and weakened state, would inev-
itably succumb. We asked to be taken into Taklakot,
but our guard refused, and in the mean time the Jong Pen

A MESSENGER OF BAD NEWS

of Taklakot had sent other messengers and soldiers to
insure the fulfilment of his orders, and to prevent our
further progress.

Our guard, now strengthened by the Taklakot men,
compelled us to leave the Taklakot track, and we began

our journey towards the cold Lumpiya. This was murder, and the Tibetans, well knowing it, calculated on telling the Indian authorities that we had died a natural death on the snows.

We were informed that we should be left at the point where the snows began, that the Tibetans would give us no food, no clothes and no blankets, and that we should be abandoned to our own devices. This, needless to say, meant certain death.

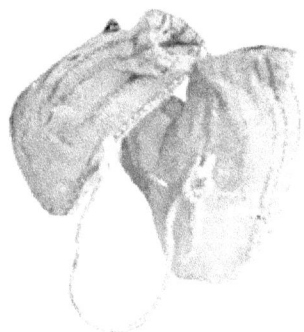

We determined to stand no more, and to play our last card. After travelling some two and a half miles westward of the Taklakot track, we declined to proceed any more in that direction. We said that, if they attempted to force us on, we were prepared to fight our guard, as whether we died by their swords and matchlocks, or frozen to death on the Lumpiya, was quite immaterial to us.

SHEEP LOADS FOR BORAX AND GRAIN

The guard, in perplexity, decided to let us halt there for the night, so as to have time to send a messenger to Taklakot to inform the Jong Pen, and ask for further instructions.

During the night the order came that we must pro-

A SHOKA-TIBETAN HALF-CASTE

ceed, so the next morning our guard prepared to start us again towards the Lumpiya. Then we three semi-corpses collected what little strength remained in us, and suddenly made an attack on them with stones; whereupon, incredible as it may seem, our cowardly guard turned tail and

A JUMLI SHED

bolted! We went on in the direction of Taklakot, followed at a distance by these ruffians, who were entreating us to make no further resistance and to go with them where they wanted us to go. If we did not, they said, they would all have their heads cut off. We refused to listen to them, and kept them away by throwing stones at them.

We had gone but a few miles when we met with a large force of soldiers and Lamas, despatched by the Jong Pen to prepare for our death. Unarmed, wounded, starved and exhausted as we were, it was useless attempting to fight against such odds. As it was, when they saw we were at liberty, they made ready to fire on us.

The Jong Pen's Chief Minister, a man called Lapsang, and the Jong Pen's Private Secretary, were at the head of this party. I went to shake hands with them and held

LAPSANG AND THE JONG PEN'S PRIVATE SECRETARY

a long and stormy palaver, but they kept firm and insisted on our turning away from the frontier, now that we were almost within a stone's-throw of it, and we must perforce proceed by the high Lumpiya Pass. Those were the Jong Pen's orders, and they, as well as I, must obey them. They would not give us or sell us either animals

"WE ATTACKED OUR GUARD WITH STONES."

or clothes, which even the small sum of money I had on me would have been sufficient to buy; and they would not provide us with even an ounce of food. We emphatically protested, and said we preferred to die where we were. We asked them to kill us then and there, for we would not budge an inch westwards.

Lapsang and the Jong Pen's Private Secretary now cunningly suggested that I should give them in writing the names of the Shokas who had accompanied me to Tibet, probably with the object of confiscating their land and goods. As I said I could not write Tibetan or Hindustani, they requested me to do it in English. This I did, but substituting for the names of my men and my signature sarcastic remarks, which must have caused the Tibetans some surprise when they had the document translated.

As, however, they refused to kill us there and then, and as Lapsang showed us great politeness and asked us to go by the Lumpiya Pass as a personal favor to him, I reluctantly decided to accept their terms rather than waste any more time, now that we were so near British soil.

Escorted by this large force of men, we had nearly reached Kardam when, in the nick of time, a horseman came up at full gallop and hailed our party. We stopped, and the man overtook us and handed Lapsang a letter. It contained an order to bring us immediately into Taklakot.

We retraced our steps along the undulating plateau above the Gakkon River, and late at night we reached the village of Dogmar, a peculiar settlement in a valley between two high cliffs of clay, the natives of which live in holes pierced in the cliff.

Lapsang, the Jong Pen's Private Secretary, and the

greater portion of their soldiers, having changed their ponies, went on to Taklakot; but we were made to halt here, when yet another letter came from the Jong Pen saying he had changed his mind and we must, after all, go by the Lumpiya Pass!

DURING the night there was a great commotion in the
place, the people running about and shouting, and a large
number of ponies with their riders arriving.

Tibet is farmed out, so to speak, to officials who have
become small feudal kings, and these are generally at log-
gerheads among themselves. To this regal jealousy, and
to disputes over the rights of the road, was due the appearance of this new army. There were altogether some
hundred and fifty men armed with matchlocks and swords.
The chieftain of this band came to me with eight or ten
other officers, and spoke so excitedly that I feared there
was trouble in store for us. There was indeed. These
new arrivals were officers and soldiers from Gyanema,
Kardam, and Barca, and they had come with strict orders
from the Barca Tarjum that we were on no account to
traverse his province or to cross by the Lumpiya Pass.
This was very amusing and tantalizing, for we had now
no way across the frontier open to us. Our guard and
some of the Jong Pen's men who had remained behind,
finding they were in the minority, thought it prudent to
eclipse themselves; and I, anxious as I naturally was to
get out of the country as quickly as possible, approved of
all that the Gyanema men said, and urged them to fight
in case the Jong Pen still insisted on my going through

the Tarjum's province.   All ways out of the country were
barred to us, and unless we resorted to force, I felt we
would never escape at all.

The Gyanema men asked me whether I would lead
them in case of a fight with the Jong Pen's soldiers; and

JUMLI TRADER AND HIS WIFE IN TIBET

I, though not very confident of their courage, accepted
the post of general-in-chief *pro tem.*, Chanden Sing and
Mansing being promoted there and then to be my aides-
de-camp. We spent the greater part of the night in ar-
ranging our plan of attack on the Jong Pen's troops, and

CLIFF HABITATIONS

when all was properly settled, the Tibetans, to show their gratitude, brought me a leg of mutton, some *tsamba*, and two bricks of tea.

The morning came, and I was given a fine pony to ride, as were also Chanden Sing and Mansing. Then, followed by my Tibetan troops — a grand cavalcade — we started gayly towards Taklakot. We had been informed that the

CHOKDENS NEAR TAKLAKOT

Jong Pen was concentrating his men at a certain point on the road to bar our way—and it was this point that we must force. My Tibetans said that they hated the Jong Pen's men, and swore they would slaughter them all if they made any stand.

"But they are such cowards," declared one of the Tibetan officers, "that they will run away."

All this talk stopped suddenly when we heard the distant tinkling of our enemies' horse-bells, and though I encouraged my men as best I could, a panic began to spread among them. The Jong Pen's men came in sight, and presently I witnessed the strange spectacle of two armies face to face, each in mortal terror of the other.

Notwithstanding my remonstrances, matchlocks and swords were deposited on the ground with anxious eagerness by both parties, to show that only peaceful intentions prevailed. Then a conference was held, in which everybody seemed ready to oblige everybody else except me.

While this was still proceeding, a horseman arrived with a message from the Jong Pen, and at last, to everybody's satisfaction, permission was granted for us to proceed into Taklakot.

My army retraced its steps towards the northwest, and, deposed from my high military post, which I had occupied only a few hours, I became again a private individual and a prisoner. With a large escort we were taken along the Gakkon, by barren cliffs and on a rocky road. We passed hundreds of *Chokdens* large and small, mostly painted red, and *mani* walls. Then, having descended by a precipitous track on whitish clay-soil, we reached a thickly inhabited district, where stone houses were scattered all over the landscape. We saw on our left the large monastery of Delaling and, a little way off, the Gomba of Sibling: then, describing a sweeping curve among stones and boulders, we rounded the high, graceful cliff, on the top of which towered the fort and monasteries of Taklakot.

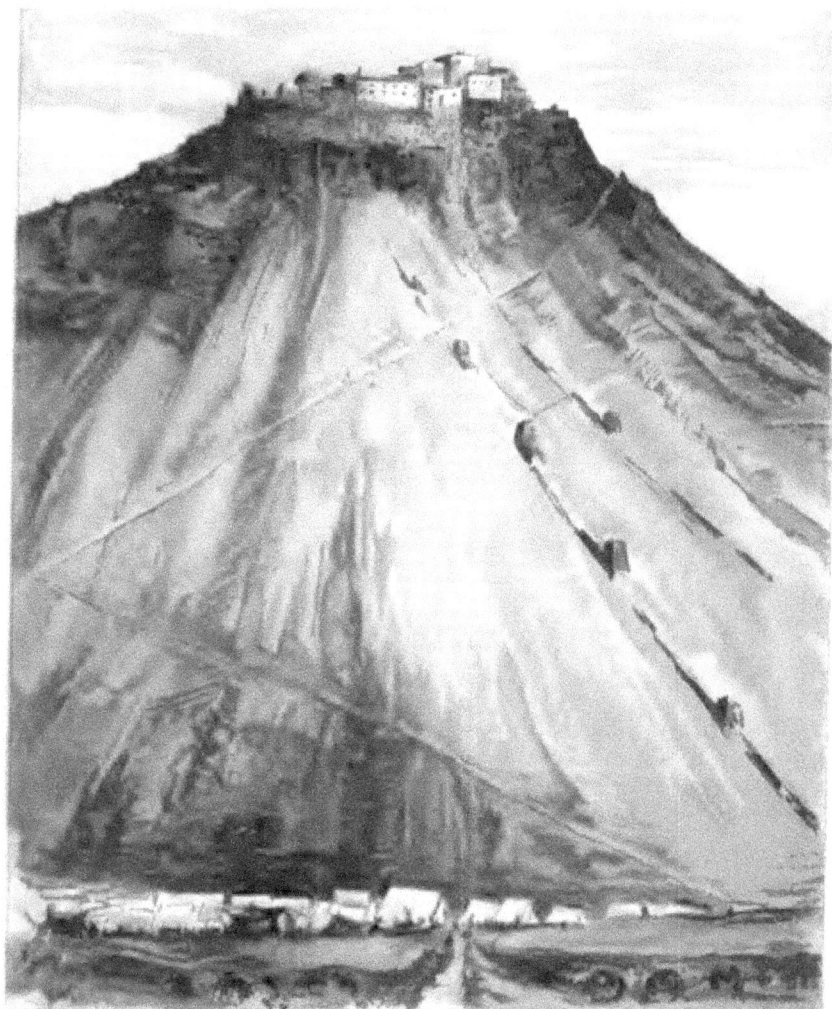

Lithographed by F. A. Brockhaus. Leipzig (Germany).

TAKLAKOT FORT.

SUCH was our anxiety, when we reached this point, lest something should happen and we should be taken back again, that, as soon as we were across the wooden bridge over the Gakkon, Chanden Sing and I, on perceiving the large Shoka encampment at the foot of the hill, lashed our ponies and ran away from our guard. Thus, galloping our hardest along the high cliff, where hundreds of people live in holes in the clay, we found ourselves at last among friends again. The Shokas, who had come over to this market to exchange their goods with the Tibetans, were astounded when they saw us, recognizing us at first with difficulty.

We inquired at once, of course, for Dr. Wilson, and when we found him the good man could, himself, barely recognize us, so changed were we. He seemed deeply moved at seeing our condition.

When the news of our arrival spread in camp, we met with the greatest kindness at the hands of everybody. In a corner of Wilson's tent was a large quantity of candied sugar—several pounds; and so famished was I that I quickly devoured the lot. Later, my Shoka friends brought in all kinds of presents in the shape of eatables which Rubso, the doctor's cook, was set to prepare.

The Political Peshkar, Karak Sing, hurried to me with a change of clothes, and other garments were given me by Dr. Wilson. My own ragged attire was literally swarming with vermin; our guard had not allowed us a single change of raiment, nor would they even hear of our washing. It was by a very special favor and on account of its sanctity that we were allowed to plunge in the sacred Mansarowar Lake.

Later in the day my wounds and injuries were examined by Dr. Wilson, who sent his reports to the Government of India, to the Commissioner of Kumaon, and to the Deputy Commissioner of Almora.

Tenderly nursed by Wilson and Karak Sing, and having partaken of plenty of good food, I found my spirits, which had fallen rather low, reviving as if by magic; and, strange to say, after a few hours of happiness, I was already beginning to forget the hardships and suffering I had endured. I remained three days at Taklakot, during which time part of my confiscated baggage was returned by the Tibetans, and, as can well be imagined, I was overjoyed to discover that among the things thus recovered were my diary, note-books, maps, and sketches. My firearms, some money, the ring I have before referred to as having been a gift of my mother's, several mathematical instruments, collections, over 400 photographic negatives, and various other articles were still missing,* but I was glad to get back as much as I did.

PUNDIT GOBARIA

* Some of the articles missing were some months later recovered by the Government of India. See Appendix.

THE AUTHOR, FEBRUARY, 1897   THE AUTHOR OCTOBER, 1897

DR. WILSON

To Dr. Wilson's tent came the Tokchim Tarjum, of
whom I give a portrait, his private secretary Nerba, whom
the reader may remember as having played an important
part in my tortures, the Jong Pen's secretary, and old
Lapsang in a fine green velvet coat with ample sleeves.
As can be seen by perusing the Government Enquiry and

DR. WILSON

Report in the Appendix to this book, the above-mentioned
Tibetan officers admitted before the Political Peshkar, Dr.
Wilson, Pundit Gobaria, and many Shokas, that the account I gave of my tortures—identical with the one in
these pages—was correct in every detail. They even professed to be proud of what they had done, and used ex-

pressions not at all flattering to the British Government, which they affected to treat with great contempt.

I nearly got the Political Peshkar and the Doctor into a scrape; for my blood, the little I had left, was boiling with rage at hearing the Tibetan insults. The climax

KARAK SING, THE POLITICAL PESHKAR

came when Nerba refused to give back my mother's ring, which he had upon him. In a passion I seized a knife that was lying by me, and leaped upon Nerba, the ruffian who, besides, had fired at me and had held me by the hair while my eyes were being burned prior to my abortive execution. Wilson and Karak Sing seized and disarmed me, but there was a general stampede of the Tibetan officers,

"'I TOLD YOU,' EXCLAIMED THE OLD SAVAGE, 'THAT WHOEVER
VISITS THE HOME OF THE RAOTS WILL HAVE MISFORTUNE.'"

A PICTURESQUE BIT OF ALMORA

and thus our interview and negotiations were brought to
an abrupt end.

In further conversation I now learned how my release
had been brought about. Dr. Wilson and the Political
Peshkar, having received the news that my servants and
myself had been beheaded, proceeded across the frontier
to make inquiries and try to recover my property. They

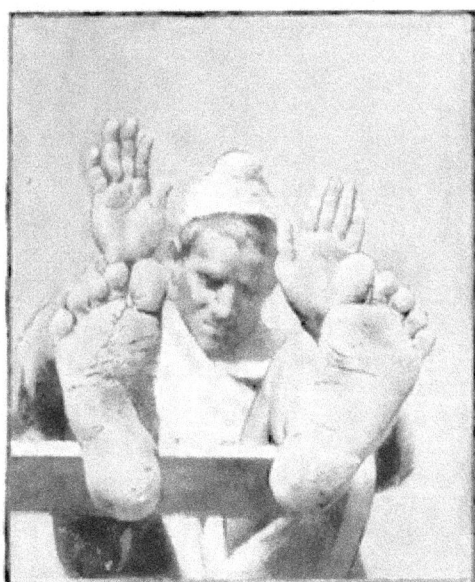

MANSING SHOWING CUTS UNDER HIS FEET

heard then from the man Suna, whom I had sent from
Mansarowar with my message, that I was still a prisoner,
covered with wounds, in rags and starving. They had
not men enough to force their way farther into the country to come and meet me; besides, the Tibetans watched
them carefully; but they, together with Pundit Gobaria,
made strong representations to the Jong Pen of Taklakot,
and, by threatening him that an army would be sent up

if I were not set at liberty, they at last obtained from the
reluctant Master of the fort* a permission that I should
be brought into Taklakot. The permission was afterwards withdrawn, but was at last allowed to be carried
into execution, and it is entirely due to the good offices
and energy of these three gentlemen that I am to-day
alive and safe — though not
yet sound.

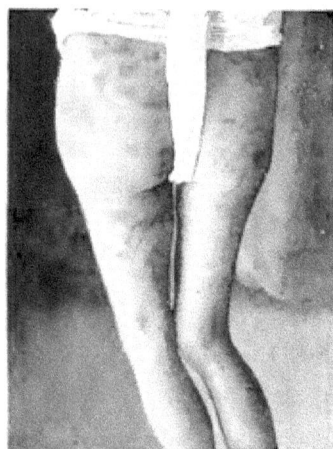

CHANDEN SING'S LEGS, SHOWING
MARKS OF LASHES AND
WOUNDS HEALED

Pundit Gobaria, who will be
remembered as having been
mentioned in my early chap-
ters, is the most influential
Shoka trader in Bhot, and on
very friendly terms with the
Tibetans. He was the inter-
mediary through whom ne-
gotiations were carried on
for my immediate release, and
it was largely owing to his
advice to the Jong Pen that
they resulted satisfactorily.

After a brief rest to recover
sufficient strength, I recom-
menced the journey towards India, and, having crossed
the Lippu Pass (16,780 feet), found myself at last again
on British soil. We descended by slow stages to Gungi,
where, in Dr. Wilson's dispensary, I had to halt for a few
days on account of my weak condition.

Wilson had here a quantity of my baggage, instruments,
camera, plates, etc., which I had discarded at the beginning of my journey, and I immediately had photographs
taken of my two servants and myself, showing our wounds

* Jong Pen = Master of the fort.

and our shocking general condition. Photographs of my
feet, taken more than a month after I had been untied
from the rack, showed a considerable swelling, as well as
the scars round the ankle and on the foot where the
ropes had cut into my flesh. In the full-face photograph
here reproduced can be noticed the injuries to my left
eye, as well as the marks of the hot iron on the skin of
my forehead and nose. Chanden Sing's legs, which were
photographed on the same occasion, though now practically healed, were still much swollen, and the marks
can be seen in the illustration where big patches of skin
and flesh had been torn away by the lashes, producing
nasty wounds.

CIVILIZATION ONCE MORE—PARALYSIS—THE TINKER PASS IN NEPAL—
KINDLY NATIVES—MR. LARKIN—GOVERNMENT INQUIRY—BACK TO
TIBET—FINAL GOOD-BYE TO THE FORBIDDEN LAND—THE RETURN
JOURNEY—FAREWELL TO MANSING—HOME AGAIN

IT was really wonderful how soon we began to pick up again under the good care of Dr. Wilson and the influence of proper food and clothing. When I saw my face for the first time in a looking-glass, I nearly had a fit, so ghastly did it look; but I felt more like myself when I had shaved off my beard of several months' growth; and, after the ever-obliging Wilson, with a pair of blunt scissors, had spent a whole afternoon in performing the functions of hairdresser, I began to look almost civilized again. Clothes were a great nuisance at first, but I soon got into the way of wearing them.

MR. J. LARKIN

The injuries to my spine were severe, and gave me much trouble. At times the whole of my left side became as if paralyzed. Besides, I invariably experienced the greatest difficulty in sitting down when I had been standing, and in getting up when I had been sitting down. Through the great strain they had undergone, my joints continued stiff and swollen, and remained so for months. I could see comparatively

ON THE LIPPU PASS

MR. LARKIN LOOKING OUT FOR THE JONG PEN FROM THE LIPPU PASS

well with my right eye, but was unable to use the left
at all.

When slightly better I made an excursion to Tinker, in
Nepal, there being a pass in the neighborhood I had not
visited. Having crossed into Nepal at Chongur, I followed a course towards 86° (b. m.), until we came to the
Zirri River, descending precipitously between high snowy
ridges. Then I kept on the right bank of the Tinker
River, first through forests of firs, then among barren

CHANDEN SING AND MANSING ENJOYING THEIR FIRST MEAL ACCORDING
TO THE RULES OF THEIR CASTES

rocks and along ravines, the track being extremely bad in
some places. The general direction was 88° (b. m.), until
the Tinker bridge was reached, by which the stream was
crossed, from which point I travelled some three miles to
74° (b. m.), and arrived at the Tinker village, a few houses
of Shokas perched on this slope of the mountain, having
for a background the magnificent snowy peaks dividing
Nepal from Tibet. From the village the track to the pass
is easy, first to 78° 30′ (b. m.), as far as the Zentim bridge,
two miles off, where the Dongon River, descending from

106 (b. m.), meets the Zeyan Yangti,* and, following the
latter stream for another four miles, one reaches the
Tinker Pass, the distance between here and Taklakot

A SHAKY PASSAGE ON THE NERPANI ROAD

being twelve miles. At 106 (b. m.) I observed a very
high snowy peak, the Dongon.

Having seen all that I wanted to see here I made my
way back to Garbyang with all speed, as I was anxious to
return to Europe as soon as possible, and I travelled

* Yangti = River.

TINKER IN NEPAL.

down to Askote in company of Peshkar Karak Sing. The Nerpani road had fallen in two or three places, and rough shaky bridges had been constructed across the deep precipices, one of which can be seen in the accompanying illustration. We met with a hearty reception everywhere, and kindness after kindness was showered upon us by all alike.

VIEW OF ASKOTE—SHOWING RAJIWAR'S PALACE

At Askote I was the guest of the good old Rajiwar, in whose garden I encamped, and who bestowed upon me every conceivable care and attention. Mr. J. Larkin, hastily despatched by the Government of India to conduct an inquiry into my case, met me there, and, though still suffering much pain, I insisted on turning back once more towards Tibet, to help him in his task. By quick marches we reached Garbyang, where a deputation of Shokas, who had returned from Tibet, came to me. Mr.

Larkin having gone on ahead. Among them I noticed several of the men who had betrayed me, and as I was told that there was no way of punishing them for their treachery, I took justice into my own hands, proceeding with a stout stick to teach them some idea of faithfulness,

SNAP-SHOT OF SHOKA VILLAGERS BEING ROUTED

whereupon the whole village ran up to get the fellows out of my clutches. Encouraged by the Tibetans, the Shokas made some insulting remarks about Englishmen; so the fight became general until, ill as I was, and alone against some hundred and fifty men, I succeeded in routing them. The thing might justly be doubted had I not been able to take a snap-shot of them as they fled helter-skelter.

Soon after leaving Garbyang, I overtook Mr. Larkin,

A TIBETAN TEMPORARY SHED

and we climbed towards the snows. We intended crossing over the Lippu Pass into Tibet to give the Jong Pen
an opportunity of being interviewed, but he refused to
meet us.

All the same, to give the Tibetans every chance, we
climbed over the Lippu Pass. It had been snowing

DR. WILSON, MYSELF, MR. LARKIN, THE POLITICAL PESHKAR, AND
JAGAT SING READY TO ASCEND THE LIPPU PASS

heavily and it was very cold. A Shoka had only a few
days previously been lost in the snow in trying to cross
over, and had been frozen to death. We waited impa-
tiently on the Tibetan side of the boundary for the Jong
Pen or his deputies, to whom letters had been sent, to
come and meet us; but they did not put in an appearance,
so in the afternoon of October 12 I definitely turned my
back on the Forbidden Land. I was still far from well.

but was glad, indeed, at the prospect of seeing England and my friends again.

We returned to our camp, a few hundred feet lower than the pass, where we had left our baggage and our men, who had suffered much from mountain sickness.

It was at this camp that the accompanying photograph, which represents me bathing at 16,300 feet, was taken by Mr. Larkin. Chanden Sing, having broken the ice in a

THE LAST GLANCE AT THE FORBIDDEN LAND

stream, poured water from a brass vessel over me, standing, with my feet on snow, in a high wind and with the temperature at 12° Fahr. I reproduce it to show that even in my reduced condition I was able to stand an unusual degree of cold. As a matter of fact, the water that had been taken from under the ice immediately froze on my shoulders, with the result that in a second I had icicles hanging on each side of my neck and a shawl of ice over my shoulders.

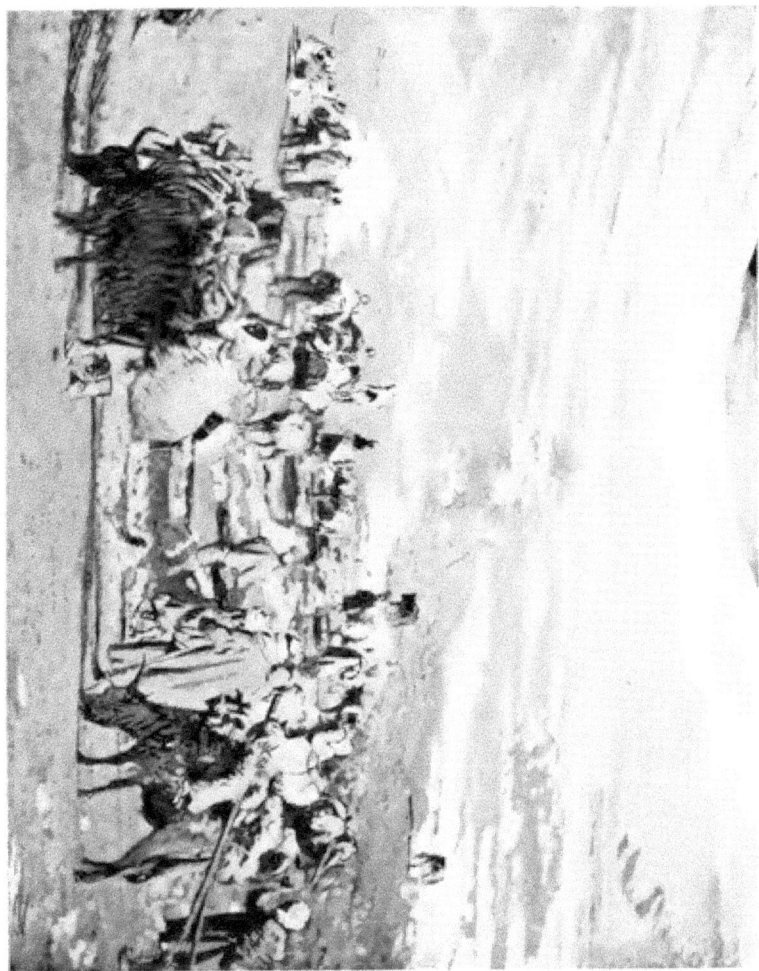

MR. LARKIN'S PARTY AND MINE HALTING NEAR THE LIPPU PASS

Having fulfilled our mission, Mr. Larkin and I returned by very quick marches to Almora; and it was a great satisfaction to me that in conducting the government inquiry in an open court, Mr. Larkin was able to obtain ample testimony from Shokas and Tibetans as to my treatment, all of which was duly reported to the Government of India,

BATHING AT 16,300 FEET

and also to the Foreign Office and India Office in London. A copy of the Enquiry and Government Report will be found in the Appendix.

Winter setting in, the Shokas, who had by now all returned from Tibet, were beginning to migrate to their winter homes at Dharchula, and when we passed the settlement many were already at work repairing the fallen-down roofs of their hibernal habitations. At Askote the

old Raot who had predicted ill-luck for me when I visited
the Raots' dwelling, came to remind me of his prophecy.
"I told you," exclaimed the old savage, "that whoever
visits the home of the Raots will have misfortune," and
I photographed the old scoundrel on the spot, together

DHARCHULA. DESERTED HABITATIONS OF SHOKAS

with his mates, who listened with satisfaction to the
words that came from the lips of their prophet.

We proceeded with no delay to Almora, and from
there went straight on to Naini Tal, the summer seat of
the Government of the Northwest Provinces and Oudh,
where a conference was held on my case by the Lieu-
tenant-Governor.

Having there enjoyed the unbounded hospitality of
that able and energetic officer, Colonel Grigg, Commissioner of Kumaon, I paid off my faithful coolie Mansing,

giving him enough for a start in life. He accompanied me to Kathgodam, the terminus of the railway, and showed genuine grief when Chanden Sing and I stepped into the train. As we steamed away from the platform, he salaamed me affectionately, having previously begged that, if ever I should go back to Tibet, I would take him with me; only next time he, too, must be provided with a rifle! That was the only condition.

Chanden Sing, who remained as my servant, travelled with me to Bombay, and from there we went direct to Florence, the home of my parents, who had suffered in their anxiety at home almost as much as I did in the Forbidden Land.

RAOTS LISTENING TO THE ACCOUNT OF MY MISFORTUNES

APPENDIX

Letter from Sir William Lee Warner, C.S.I., *Political and Secret Department, India Office, London.*

♛

*" Honi soit
qui mal y pense"*

India Office, Whitehall, S.W.
August 4, 1898.

Dear Sir:

With reference to the request contained in your letter of the 27th, and to your interview with me of the same day, I forward herewith for your use a copy of Mr. Larkin's " Enquiry and report " into your treatment by the Tibetans.

Yours faithfully,

(Signed) W. Lee Warner.

A. Henry Savage Landor, Esq.

GOVERNMENT REPORT BY J. LARKIN, Esq., MAGISTRATE OF THE FIRST CLASS.

Mr. Arnold Henry Savage Landor having been reported to have been captured and tortured by the Tibetans, I was sent up to Garbyang in Byans to ascertain the facts.

Mr. Landor arrived in India on the 10th of April last. He proceeded to Almora, where he arrived on the 27th idem. He stayed there until the 10th of May, to make arrangements for his travels in Tibet. At first he was advised to take some Gurkha soldiers with him, but this fell through, as the military did not accede to his request. He then, on the 27th May, arrived in Garbyang in Byans *patti.* It appears to have been his intention

211

to have entered Tibet by the Lippu Lek Pass. This is the easiest, being about 16,780 feet above sea level. It is the most frequented route taken by the traders of Byans and Chaudans, and is adjacent to Taklakot, a mart for wood, salt, borax, grain, etc. He was, however, frustrated in this, inasmuch as the Jong Pen of Taklakot came to know of Mr. Landor's intention and took steps to prevent it. He caused bridges to be destroyed and stationed guards along the route.

Moreover, he appears to have been kept fully cognizant of Mr. Landor's moves through the agency of his spies in Garbyang.

Under these circumstances Mr. Landor was compelled to resort to some other route, and selected the Lumpia Pass, which stands at an altitude of 18,150 feet.

On the 13th July last Mr. Landor, with a following of thirty men, entered Tibet. He reached Gyanima, where he was stopped by the Barkha Tarjum. This personage, however, after some persuasion, consented to permit Mr. Landor and seven followers to go forward to the Mansarowar Lake.

Next day the accorded permission was withdrawn, and Mr. Landor and his party were turned back. The party returned three marches, when Mr. Savage Landor determined to go to Mansarowar by the unfrequented wilds.

On the 21st July Mr. Landor, with nine followers, at midnight, in a terrific snow-storm, climbed up the mountain and went off, the bulk of his party continuing their retreat to the Lumpia Lek. By this strategic move Mr. Landor baffled the Tibetan guards (Chaukidars). He carefully avoided coming into contact with any of the inhabitants, and in order to do so was obliged to keep to the high mountains and unfrequented wilds.

Travelling thus, with the aid of his compass, sextant, and sketch maps, he reached Mansarowar.

Here five of his followers declined to accompany him any farther, so he paid and dismissed them. This was at Tucker. Thus Mr. Landor was reduced to a following of four men. He went on, however, and had accomplished but three marches more when two more of his followers deserted him at night. These went off with some of his supplies, all his servants' food, and ropes.

Mr. Landor was now reduced to the following of a bearer

APPENDIX

(Chanden Sing) and a coolie (Mansing). Despite his misfortunes he determined to push on: his intention appears to have been to reach Lhassa.

He went over the Mariam La Pass.* This attains an altitude of over 16,000 feet.

Meanwhile the deserters had bruited about the information of Mr. Landor's intention of getting to Lhassa.

While crossing the Nio Tsambo River one of Mr. Landor's yaks went under. The yak was saved, but its valuable load, consisting of all the tinned provisions, Rs. 800 in cash, three pairs of shoes, one slaughtered sheep, wearing apparel, razors, skinning instruments, and some three hundred rifle cartridges, was lost.

This accident was directly the cause of Mr. Landor's capture, as he and his two followers, who were footsore, starving, and disheartened, were driven to seek food and horses from the inhabitants of the country. On the 19th of August, 1897, they went to a place called Toxem. The villagers received them well and promised to supply them with food and horses. Next morning, the 20th idem, a number of Tibetans came to Mr. Landor's tent bringing food and ponies.

While Mr. Landor and his servants were engaged in trying and selecting ponies, the crowd increased and came up behind its three victims.

Suddenly, without any warning, the Tibetans rushed on Mr. Landor and his two servants and, overwhelming them by numbers, made prisoners of them. They cruelly bound their surprised victims. Then a number of soldiers (who had lain in ambush) arrived and took over the prisoners. The first person to be dealt with was the bearer, Chanden Sing. He was accused of having taken his master into Tibet. He was questioned as to this, and also as to the maps and sketches found with Mr. Landor's things. I may mention that when the arrests were made the Tibetans took all of Mr. Landor's property, which they handled very roughly, damaging most of the things. Hearing the Tibetans accuse the bearer, Mr. Landor called out that his servant was in no way responsible for his having entered Tibet. Thereupon a Lama

* Maium Pass.

struck him (Mr. Landor) a blow on the head with the butt-end of his riding-whip. Chanden Sing was then tied down and flogged. He received two hundred lashes with whips, wielded by two Lamas. Then the prisoners were kept apart for the night, bound with cords. Next day Mr. Landor was placed on a horse, seated on a spiked pack-saddle. Mansing was put on a bare-backed horse. They still were bound. Mr. Landor's arms were secured behind his back. Thus they were taken off at a gallop towards Galshio. When the party were nearing that place they came up with a party of Lamas, awaiting them by the roadside. Here Mr. Landor's horse was whipped and urged to the front. A kneeling soldier, his musket resting on a prop, fired at Mr. Landor as he went past. The shot failed to take effect. Then they stopped the pony and fastened a long cord to Mr. Landor's handcuffs. The other end was held by a soldier on horseback. The party then continued their career, the Lamas having fallen in. While proceeding at full gallop, the horseman who held the cord attached to Mr. Landor's handcuffs pulled hard at it to try and unhorse the latter. Had this occurred Mr. Landor must have been trampled to death under the troop of horsemen behind him. Thus they hurried onward till they neared Galshio,* when at a turn in the road a soldier was seen kneeling at the "ready," who fired a shot at Mr. Landor as he came abreast of him. This, like the previous shot, missed its object.

Arriving at Galshio, Mr. Landor was torn off his pony. He was in a bleeding state, the spikes in the pack-saddle having severely wounded his back. He asked for a few minutes' respite, but was jeeringly told by his guards that it was superfluous, as he was to be beheaded in a few minutes. He was then taken, his legs stretched as far as they could be forced apart, and then tied to the sharp edge of a log shaped like a prism. The cords were bound so tightly that they cut into the flesh.

Then a person named Nerba, the secretary of the Tokchim Tarjum, seized Mr. Landor by the hair of his head, and the chief official, termed the *Pombo*, came up with a red-hot iron, which he placed in very close proximity to Mr. Landor's eyes.

* Galshio, or Gyatsho.

APPENDIX

The heat was so intense that for some moments Mr. Landor felt as if his eyes had been scorched out. It had been placed so close that it burned his nose. The *Pombo* next took a matchlock, which he rested on his victim's forehead and then discharged upwards.

The shock was consequently very much felt. Handing the empty gun to an attendant soldier, the *Pombo* took a two-handed sword. He laid the sharp edge on the side of his victim's neck as if to measure the distance to make a true blow. Then wielding the sword aloft, he made it whiz past Mr. Landor's neck. This he repeated on the other side of the neck.

After this tragic performance Mr. Landor was thrown to the ground, and a cloth put over his head and face to prevent his seeing what was being done to his servant Mansing. This must have been done to make Mr. Landor believe that Mansing was being executed. After a short time the cloth was removed, and Mr. Landor beheld his servant, with his legs stretched, tied to the same log. Mr. Landor was kept for twenty-four hours in this trying position, legs stretched as far as possible and arms bound to a pole, and Mansing for twelve hours. To add to their misery, they were kept in the rain, and were afterwards seated in a pool of water. The effect of this torture was to strain the muscles of the legs and arms and injure the spine.

When Mr. Landor's legs were unloosed from their cords, they were so numbed and swollen that for sixteen hours he did not recover the use of them and feared they were mortifying. Mr. Landor's property was overhauled by the officials of Galshio and sealed up. On the afternoon of the third day, at Galshio, the two prisoners were taken on foot to Toxem. It was a very trying march, inasmuch as several rivers had to be crossed.

On his arrival at Toxem Mr. Landor saw his bearer, Chanden Sing, in a very precarious condition, as the latter had had no food for four days. During all this time the prisoners were firmly bound and carefully guarded. Next day, Mr. Landor and Chanden Sing were placed on yaks. Mansing had to walk. Thus they were taken in the direction of Mansarowar Lake. It was only on arrival at Mansarowar that his guards unbound Mr. Landor.

Arriving at Dogmar the party were stopped by the Jong Pen

215

of Taklakot, who refused to give them passage through his district. This was a very serious affair, as it meant that the worn-out prisoners would have to be taken by a long, circuitous route *via* Gyanima and into India by the Lumpia Pass. This would probably have done for them. Owing to the intervention of the Rev. Harkua Wilson, of the Methodist Episcopal Mission, *Peshkár* Kharak Sing Pal and Pundit Gobaria, the most influential person among the Bhutias* of Byans, the Jong Pen was compelled to withdraw his prohibition and give his sanction to the prisoners being conveyed to Taklakot.

Arriving at this place the prisoners were hospitably received by the Rev. Harkua Wilson, who is also a medical man. He examined their injuries and attended to them. His statement discloses the dreadful condition he found them in. The Tibetan guards made over some of Mr. Landor's property to him at Taklakot. It was then found that much property had not been restored. Mr. Landor had a list drawn up from memory of his unrestored property. This list (a copy) was handed to the Jong Pen of Taklakot.

I append the list. The Jong Pen has been called upon to restore the missing articles. He urges that the affair did not occur in his district, and that he is in no way responsible for the loss of the property.

He has, however, promised to try to recover them, alleging that the affair has been reported to a superior authority at Gartok. From what I could gather here, it seems probable that all the missing property, save the money, will be restored. I tried to see the Jong Pen, but he pleaded illness and the inutility of a meeting in which he had nothing new to disclose. This personage is notorious in these parts for his implacable hatred to English subjects.

The account of the affair as given by Mr. Savage Landor is fully borne out by his two servants, and, moreover, the Tibetans who took part in it did not try to hide it.

In the Rev. Harkua Wilson's tent at Taklakot, before *Peshkár* Kharak Sing, Gobaria, and a large number of Bhutias, several Tibetan officials corroborated the whole account as related by

---

* Bhutias, or Shokas.

APPENDIX

Mr. Landor. The man Nerba, who had held Mr. Landor's hair when about to be beheaded and have his eyes burned out, admitted he had taken such part in the affair. There can be no doubt that the above account is true and unexaggerated, for the whole of Byans and Chaudans are ringing with it. The Jong Pen of Taklakot was given ample opportunity to explain the affair, but he declined to do so.

Mr. Savage Landor held Chinese passports, and his conduct during his stay in that country did not warrant the officials to have treated him in the barbarous, cruel way they did. I satisfied myself, by careful inquiry from the people here, as to how Mr. Landor behaved.

He is said to have been most munificent in his dealings with all, and invariably affable and courteous. I had seen Mr. Landor just before his entry into Tibet, and when I met him I could scarcely recognize him, though he had then fairly recovered from the terrible treatment he had received. I saw the marks of the cords on his hands and feet, and they are still visible after this lapse of time. He complains that he is still suffering from the injury done his spine, and fears that it may be of a permanent nature.

J. LARKIN.

October 15, 1897.

All communications to Government should give the No., date, and subject of any previous correspondence, and should note the Department quoted

From

THE UNDER-SECRETARY TO GOVERNMENT, N.-W. Provinces and Oudh.

To

A. H. SAVAGE LANDOR, Esq.,
c/o Messrs. GRINDLAY, GROOM & CO.,
Bankers, Bombay.

Political Department.

Dated ALLAHABAD, *November* 13, 1897.

SIR,

In reply to your letter of November 5, I am desired to send you a printed copy of depositions recorded by Mr. Larkin as noted below :

1. Of yourself;   2. Of Chanden Sing;
3. Of Man Sing;   4. Of Rev. Harkua Wilson;
5. Of Pundit Gobaria;   6. Of Kharak Sing;
7. Of Suna.

I have the honor to be, Sir,

Your most obedient Servant,

H. N. WRIGHT,

Under-Secretary to Government, North-Western Provinces and Oudh. N.M.

APPENDIX

ALMORA DISTRICT.

IN THE COURT OF J. LARKIN, Esq., Magistrate of the 1st class.

In re The Matter of the Tortures, Robbery, &c., of A. HENRY SAVAGE LANDOR, Esq., and his servants, by the Thibetan Authorities.

DEPOSITION OF MR. A. HENRY SAVAGE LANDOR : *taken on the 4th day of October*, 1897. *Oath administered by me.*

My name is Arnold Henry Savage Landor; my father's name is Charles Savage Landor; I am by caste European, British subject; by occupation artist and traveller; my home is at Empoli (Calappiano), police station Empoli, district Florence, Tuscany, Italy; I reside at London.

Having made up my mind to travel in Turkistan and Thibet, for geographical and scientific purposes, as well as to study the manners and customs of those people, I obtained a British passport from the Foreign Office and one from the Chinese Legation in London. I had already a passport granted me by the Chinese Government through the British Consul at Tientsin, China. I also possess letters from Lord Salisbury and the officials of the British Museum. I am prepared to submit all these for scrutiny. I arrived in India by the P. and O. ss. *Peninsular* about the beginning of April. I travelled rapidly up to Almora. I stayed there a short time to make arrangements for my travels in Thibet. I entered that country through the Lumpia Lek. I kept away from the road and paths, passing over several ranges of high mountains, camping at very high altitudes, for nearly three weeks. When I started I had thirty men with me. Twenty-one of them left me when I was only five days in. At Mansarowar Lake five Shokas declined to go any farther. I paid them up and they left. It was they who gave the Lamas of Tucker information of my intention to go to Lhassa. I had proceeded but three marches towards the Maium La Pass when my only two remaining Shokas deserted during the night. They carried off all my stock of provisions for my Hindu servants, ropes, straps, &c. My party had now dwindled down to Chanden Sing (bearer) and Man Sing (coolie). The latter was ill; I fear he is developing leprosy. His feet were in a very sore and cut condition, hence he could scarcely get along. I went over the Maium La Pass and followed the course of the Brahmaputra River for many troublesome marches, until we reached the Neo Tsambo (river), in crossing which one of my yaks sank, and its load went down and was lost. I tried hard, by diving and swimming in this very cold and rapid river, to recover my goods, but failed to do so, owing to the depth and muddiness of the water. The load contained all my provisions, some clothes, and all my shoes, cash rupees eight hundred, my lantern, some ammunition, and sundry knives and razors. This misfortune drove me to Toxem, which place we reached in a state of starvation. It had taken us several days to get there. Owing to the weak, fatigued, and starved condition of my two followers, I had to seek to get them food and horses, as it was impossible for them to get on without horses. I would not desert them, as I might have, as I was still prepared to push on despite the many difficulties I had to encounter hourly. Toxem consisted of one mud house and an encampment of about eighty tents. The shepherds received us kindly and consented to sell me horses and provisions. I encamped for the night about two miles beyond the settlement. During the evening several persons visited my encampment, bringing me gifts of provisions. I invariably gave them money in return, certainly three or four times more than the value of the articles presented. During the night I was disturbed several times, and went out into the darkness, but failed to discover any one. This, however, was my nightly experience; hence I grew to attach little moment to these noises. In the morning (August 20), two or three Thibetans came offering to sell me provisions and ponies. While I and my two servants were engaged examining and selecting ponies, I noticed that numbers of villagers came up one by one, spinning their wool or carrying bags of *tsamba* (meal), while others arrived with more ponies. My servants, overjoyed at the hope of getting mounts, rode first one pony and then another to suit themselves. Chanden Sing, having selected one, called me to see it and try it. I walked to the spot, which was about a hundred yards from my tent. Naturally I was unarmed. The demeanor of these people had been so friendly that it gave me no cause to suspect that any treachery was anticipated. While I stood with my hands behind my back, enjoying the delight of my long-suffering servants, I was suddenly seized from the back by several persons. I was seized simultaneously by the neck, arms, wrists, and legs, and was thrown down in a prone position. I fought and struggled and managed to shake off some of my captors, so that I was able to regain my feet; but others rushed up and I was quickly surrounded and overpowered by twenty-five or thirty persons. Ropes were thrown around my neck, legs, and body, and thus entangled, I was thrown three several times more to the ground. I fought with my head, teeth, legs, arms, and succeeded in regaining my legs four times. They overcame me at last by strangling me with the rope which they had thrown round my neck. Then they bound me hand, foot, and neck. When I had an opportunity to look round, I saw Chanden Sing struggling against some fifteen or twenty foes. He was quickly entangled, thrown, and secured by ropes. Even Man Sing, the weak and jaded coolie, was overcome by four stout, powerful men, though he was not able to offer any resistance. He, too, was bound. While we were struggling against our treacherous foes, some person gave a signal—a shrill whistle—which brought up an ambush of four hundred armed soldiers. These soldiers took up a position round us and covered us with their muskets. Then they searched us and rifled us of any things we had in our pockets. They next proceeded to my tent and took possession of everything I possessed. They sealed up my things in bags subsequent to having overhauled and examined them. Then with shouts and hisses they led us prisoners to Toxem. There we were separated, being placed in separate tents. Guards of many armed soldiers were placed to watch us. In the afternoon of the same day a *Pombo* (a man in authority), with several high Lamas and military officers, held a court under a gaudy tent. I saw Chanden Sing led forward to this court. I was led to the rear of the mud house to preclude my witnessing the scene. I heard Chanden Sing being interrogated in a loud, angry tone and accused of having been my guide. Next I heard Chanden Sing's moans and groans. Then a company of soldiers led me before this tribunal. I was ordered to kneel, and as I would not do so, they tried to compel me to do so by forcing me on my knees. I succeeded in maintaining a standing posture. Then I beheld my servant, Chanden Sing, lying down, stripped from the waist downward, in the midst of a number of Lamas and soldiers. I saw two stalwart Lamas, one on each side of him, castigating him with knotted leather thongs. They were laying on him with vigorous arms from his waist to his feet. He was bleeding. As I could not be compelled to kneel, I was allowed to sit down before the *Pombo's* officer. Then my note-books and printed maps were produced, and I was interrogated, first as to the route I had taken, then as to why I had drawn my maps and sketches. I explained as best I could, partly through my servant, Chanden Sing, and partly through an interpreter (a person who styled himself a Gurkha and who knew a little Hindustani. He wore the garb of the Thibetan). I explained to the officers that Chanden Sing, my servant, did not know the route or anything about the maps and sketches ; that I had brought him as my servant, and that I alone was responsible for the route taken by me, and for the maps and sketches ; that my servant was not to be punished : that I should be if anybody was punishable. Thereupon one of the Lamas struck me a hard blow on the head with the butt-end of his riding-crop, and they continued to castigate my servant, Chanden Sing. I was led away captive, but nevertheless heard the moans of my unfortunate servant. It began raining heavily, and I was taken to a tent, where I was cruelly bound. Soldiers were placed within and without the tent to guard me. I was thus kept the greater part of the night with my arms manacled behind my back and my legs bound. I was so bound that rest or sleep was impossible. The tent was swarming with vermin, which quickly covered me ; and I may here remark that I suffered unspeakable tortures from this pest all the time I was in captivity, as I was never permitted to wash, bathe, or change my clothes. In the tent my guard lighted a fire of yak's dung, and the tent was filled with a suffocating smoke, which wellnigh choked me. I was placed near a heap of this stinking fuel. I must say that it was a night full of indescribable misery for me. Though I was fasting all that day and night, yet my cruel jailers gave me no food. I was thus kept a prisoner the following day until 4 P.M. Then a soldier entered the tent and informed me that I was to be flogged, my legs broken, my eyes burnt out, and then beheaded. I merely laughed at him; I could not but think that this was said merely to intimidate me. Half an hour later another person arrived and signalled to my guard to lead me out. Not considering me sufficiently secure already, they tightened my bonds and tied others round my body. In this fashion I was taken to the sole house (mud one) in the encampment. Here an enormous pair of heavy handcuffs were put on my hands, which were still kept behind my back. Even in this the treachery of my captors was shown, for they patted me on the back and called me a good man, and told me I was to be taken back to Taklakot. This they said fearing I would resist. Then, after locking the handcuffs, they made the key over to one person, who rode away quickly with it, lest I might possibly manage to get the key and unlock my handcuffs. For this reason I was never permitted to see or know who carried the key. Just then I heard the voice of my servant, Chanden Sing, calling to me in a very weak tone. He said: "*Hazur! Hazur! Hum murjaiega!*" I endeavored to get to the poor wretch's assistance. Upon my trying to move towards him my several guards sprang upon me and ruthlessly grappled me and threw me on to the back of a horse. I could only call aloud to my poor servant that I was being taken to Taklakot that day, and that he would be brought after me the following day. I noticed that Chanden Sing was roughly seized and hurled back into one of the rooms of the house, so that we could hold no conversation. My other servant, Man Sing, had his arms pinioned, and he was put on a bare-backed pony. The saddle of the horse I had been thrown upon is worthy of description. It was merely the wooden frame of a very high-backed saddle. From this high, projecting back or crupper four or five sharp iron spikes were sticking out. These caught me on the small of my back. My guard was then augmented by some twenty or thirty mounted soldiers with muskets and swords. My pony was held by a horseman, who rode before me. We set off at a furious gallop. Thus we travelled for miles until we arrived at a spot where the *Pombo* with a following of

Lamas, banner-men, and soldiers, some two hundred in all, were drawn up. Here my pony was allowed to go on first, and the others reined up and drew aside. As I passed before the *Pombo* and his following, a person named Nerba (the Private Secretary of the Tokchim Tarjum) deliberately knelt and fixed his musket on its rest and fired at me from a few paces. The bullet whizzed past me. I was still at a gallop, which no doubt saved my life, as the marksman could not take a steady aim. My pony took fright and reared and plunged, but I maintained my seat, though I was being cruelly pricked by the spikes in the crupper. My pony was then seized and a long cord with a swivel at the end was fastened to my handcuffs. The cord was about fifty yards long. The other end was held by a horseman. In this way we all set off at a hard gallop, and in order to accelerate the speed, a horseman rode by my side and he lashed my pony furiously to make it go at its hardest; meanwhile the horseman who held the cord did his utmost to pull me out of the saddle, so that I would have of a certainty been trampled to death by the cohort behind me. While thus riding furiously with my arms extended backwards I had the flesh rubbed off my hands and knuckles, so much so that the bone was exposed in places, and as the horseman at the back tugged to get me off and I clung hard with my knees, every tug brought me into forcible contact with the spikes in the crupper and wounded me cruelly. The cord was one made of yak's hair. It was strong, but it eventually gave way. The shock unhorsed the soldier. I was all but thrown. This ludicrous incident provoked much mirth among my guards. They stopped my pony and the runaway steed of the dismounted cavalier. The cord was retied with sundry strong knots, and after an interruption of a few minutes we resumed our break-neck gallop, I being in front. When nearing Galshio, and as I was going round the curve of a sand-hill, a soldier, who had been posted in ambush, fired a shot at me from a few paces distant. The shot did not strike me. This incident did not stop our headlong career, and we continued on until we arrived at Galshio about sunset. This was the 21st August last. At this place there is a large monastery on the crown of a low hill. At some distance from the base of the hill, and on the plain, was pitched the large white tent of the *Pombo*. Our cavalcade drew up there. I was then roughly torn out of my saddle by two or three men. I requested to stop for one moment. My captors refused me this, and, roughly thrusting me forward, said that as I was about to be beheaded in an instant, it was unnecessary. I was hustled to the left front of the tent, where, on the ground, lay a log of wood in the shape of a prism. Upon the sharp edge of it I was made to stand. I was held by the body by several persons, while others pulled my legs as wide apart as they could be stretched. Then my feet were very securely tied by cords of yak-hair. The cords were so tight that they cut into the flesh in numerous places, some of the cuts or wounds being about three inches long. When I was thus secured one ruffian (Nerba), whom I have alluded to above, came forward and seized me by the hair of my head. He pulled my hair as hard as he could. My hair was long, as I had not had it cut since the day preceding my departure from London, about the middle of March. The others formed up in front of me in a semicircle. Then the *Pombo* arose and was handed a bar of iron, which had been made red hot in a brazier, the end grasped by the *Pombo* being bound round with red cloths. He strode up to me, urged on by the Lamas, and said, jeeringly, that as I had gone to see the country, my punishment would be to have my eyes burnt out. This was in allusion to what I had said at Toxem—viz., that I was a traveller and merely wished to see the country. He then placed the red-hot bar of iron parallel to and about an inch and a half or two inches from my eyeballs, and all but touching the nose. The heat was so intense that it seemed as if my eyes were desiccated and my nose scorched. There is still a mark of the burn on my nose. I was forced to shut my eyes instinctively. He seemed to me to have kept the bar of heated iron before my eyes for fully thirty seconds or so. After some moments I opened my eyes and beheld the hot iron on the ground. I saw him take a musket from the hands of one of the soldiers standing by. He placed this against my forehead and discharged it upwards, giving me a severe shock, though nothing worse. Handing back the discharged weapon to the soldier, the *Pombo* seized his long two-handed sword and came at me. He swung it from side to side, all the time foaming from his mouth. This foaming, I believe, was produced artificially. He then motioned to the man who all this time held me by the hair of my head to bend my neck. I resisted with all my might to keep my head erect. Then the *Pombo* touched my neck with the sharp blade of his sword as if to measure the distance for a clean, effective stroke. Then he raised the sword and made a blow at me with all his might. The sword passed disagreeably close to my neck, but did not touch me. I did not flinch; and my cool, indifferent demeanor seemed to impress him, so much so that he seemed reluctant to continue his diabolical performance; but the *posse* of Lamas urged him on by gesticulations and vociferous shouts. Thereupon he went through the same performance on the other side of my neck. This time the blade passed so near that I felt that the blow had not been more than half an inch from my neck. This terminated the sword exercise, much to the disgust of the Lamas, who still continued to urge the swordsman on. Then they held an excited consultation. About this time my coolie, Man Sing, who had frequently fallen off his bare-backed pony, arrived. The person who held my hair then relinquished his hold, and another person came up and gave me a forcible push, which gave me a nasty fall on my back, straining all the tendons of my legs. Then my servant, Man Sing, was brought forward and tied by his legs to the same log of wood to which I was fastened. Then they made it appear that they were going to behead Man Sing. I was pushed up into a sitting posture and a cloth thrown over my head and face, so that I could not see what was being enacted. I heard Man Sing groan, and I concluded he had been despatched. I was left in this terrible suspense for about a quarter of an hour. Then the cloth was removed, and I beheld my servant lying before me bound to the log. We both asked for food. This seemed to amuse our torturers, for they laughed. In the meanwhile the day was beginning to wane, and our jailers made us understand that our execution was merely put off to the following day. After some time *tsamba* (meal) and tea were brought in, and it was stuffed into our mouths by our captors. We were kept out in the open without any shelter from the pouring rain. We were sitting in one or two inches of rain and were drenched and numbed with cold. I have already said my hands were manacled from the back; so also were Man Sing's. But at nightfall our captors increased our tortures by straining our man-

acled arms upwards as high as they could be forced, and then secured them to an upright pole at the back. This caused very severe pain, straining the spine in an incredible way. Then they tied
a cord from Man Sing's neck to mine, the effect of which was to
make us maintain a most painful position. A guard encircled us,
and with them were two watch-dogs tied to pegs. The guard
were apparently so confident of our not being able to escape that
they drew their heavy blankets over their heads and slept. One
of them left his sword lying by his side. This made me conceive
the daring plan to try to escape. Knowing the extremely supple nature of my hands, I succeeded in drawing the right hand
out of my handcuffs. After an hour's anxious and stealthy work
I managed to unloose Man Sing's bonds round his feet. In his
joy at feeling partly free, Man Sing moved his legs rather clumsily, which the vigilant watch-dogs detected and gave the alarm
by barking. The guard were aroused. They went and fetched
a light and examined our fastenings. I had succeeded in replacing my hand inside the handcuff. They found Man Sing's bonds
loose, and, giving him a few cuts with a whip, warned him that
if he undid them again they would decapitate him, and refast-
ened them. Then they placed the light between us and put a
shelter overhead to prevent the rain extinguishing the light. At
about 6 or 7 A.M. the following day they undid Man Sing's feet.
I was kept all that day until sunset in the same uncomfortable
and painful posture. Thus I was kept fully twenty-four hours.
During the day my property had been overhauled and sealed.
One of the Lamas picked up my Henri-Martini rifle and put a
cartridge in the breach, but failed to push it home firmly. He
then discharged the gun. The muzzle of the barrel burst and
the face of the Lama was much injured thereby. I laughed
heartily at this, and this apparently amused the *Pombo*, for he,
too, joined in. About half an hour after this incident my feet
were untied. It was then sunset. I found I had lost the use of
my feet. It took my right foot some two or three hours before
the blood began to circulate freely, but my left foot remained
like dead until the following day. That night my feet were secured by cords. A bowl of some boiling, steaming liquid, which
I was informed was tea, was presented to me to drink. The
eagerness of the surrounding Lamas that I should partake of it

aroused my suspicion. When it was pushed up to my lips I merely sipped it and declined it. After a short time I felt most sharp, excruciating pains in my stomach, which continued for several days. I could not but conclude that the drink proffered had been poisoned. The following day Man Sing and I were led back on foot to Toxem, our jailers riding on horses. We had to go at a great speed despite our severely lacerated feet. We crossed several cold streams, sinking in mud and water to the waist. At Toxem, to my great delight, I beheld Chanden Sing still alive. We were detained there for that night. On the following day we were placed on yaks' backs and hurried off towards Taklakot. Thus we journeyed at an unpleasantly fast pace for fifteen days, from before daybreak to nightfall. Our guards were bent on taking us *via* the Lumpia Pass; but as this meant a long, protracted journey of fifteen or sixteen days, over ice and snow, I knew that we would, in our starved, weakened state, succumb. We were all but naked. This was a day's journey on this side of Mansarowar, where our bonds had been unloosed. We rebelled, and it wellnigh ended in a fight, but our guards consented to halt at Dogmar, until they sent to inquire if the Jong Pen of Taklakot would give us passage through his jurisdiction. After much demur we were eventually taken to Taklakot. This arrangement, I subsequently learnt, was entirely due to the good offices and energy of the *Political Peshkár* Kharak Sing Pal, Rev. H. Wilson, and Pundit Gobaria. On arriving at Taklakot we hastened to Rev. Harkua Wilson's tent, where we were warmly received, attended to, fed, and clothed. My injuries were examined by the Rev. Harkua Wilson, who is a hospital assistant, and who will be able to depose to their nature and extent. In this gentleman's tent, and in the hearing of several persons, among whom were *Peshkár* Kharak Sing, Rev. H. Wilson, and Pundit Gobaria, the man Nerba, above mentioned, the Toxem Tarjum, and the Jong Pen's secretary, and also Lapsang, chief secretary to the Jong Pen, admitted that my account of the affair was perfectly true. Some of my property, more or less damaged, was then restored me by the Tokchim Tarjum. I then gave him two lists, one showing articles restored me, and the other the articles missing. The *Peshkár* Kharak Sing has copies of the lists. I was in a very weak state, very exhausted

APPENDIX

through what I had suffered and little food. It was due to the kind, liberal, and attentive care and treatment of the Rev. H. Wilson and *Peshkár* Kharak Sing Pal that I recovered. The few ragged clothes I had on were literally swarming with lice, as I had no change of raiment, nor was I ever allowed to wash. I contracted the vermin from the tents I was kept in and also from my guards who at first slept round me.

Read over to witness.   J. LARKIN.

A. HENRY SAVAGE LANDOR

DEPOSITION OF CHANDEN SING, *taken on the 9th day of October,* 1897.

Solemn affirmation administered by me.

My name is Chanden Sing; my father's name is Bije Singh; I am by caste Thatola; thirty-two years of age; by occupation *kheti;* my home is at That, police station Bisot, district Almora.

I took service as a bearer with Mr. Landor at Almora on the 27th or 28th April last. I accompanied him on his trip to Thibet. We went along through the wilds, encountering many hardships and reached Toxem. There I insisted on my master buying ponies to take us to Darjeeling. This resulted in our capture, for up to then we had vigilantly kept away from the people. The people who brought us ponies to buy played us false. They informed the authorities, who sent soldiers, who lay in ambush behind the sandhills until the crowd of horse-dealers and lookers-on, whom we did not suspect of treachery, surrounded and seized us. We were bound with cords by the arms (at back) and legs. My master was more cruelly tied than we two servants. We were taken to the Rája,* who accused me of having brought my master into the country. I was then stretched out and two strong men with whips inflicted two hundred stripes on me. I was questioned as to the maps. My master called out that he, not I, alone understood them, and asked that I should not be beaten. Thereupon a Lama struck him across the head and removed him to a distance, so that I could not communicate with

* Raja, or King.

229

him. They took all our property. Then we were kept separate for the night. I was put in a room and my hands tied to a pole. I could not sleep with the pain I was in. Next day my master, with his hands tied behind his back, was put on a spiked saddle and tied by a long rope held by a horseman. He went at a gallop surrounded by about fifty horsemen armed with guns and swords. Man Sing, our coolie, was also taken with him. My guards informed me my master was to be decapitated at Galshio, and that I was to be beheaded where I was. On the fourth or fifth day my master returned. Meanwhile I was a close prisoner, bound up without food. When I saw my master he was in a pitiful state. He was handcuffed with enormous cuffs, clothes torn to rags, bleeding from his waist, feet and hands swollen. Next day a guard on horseback took us back, bound as we were, on yaks' backs, towards Mansarowar. There I had my cords unloosed. My master was kept bound until we got to Tangchim. We were eventually taken to Taklakot, where the Rev. Harkua Wilson met us and saw our condition. He attended to our wants. My master was wellnigh at death's door. The Thibetans returned some of my master's property, but they have kept about 475 rupees in cash, two rifles, revolver, two files, a lot of soap, medicine, a butterfly dodger, matches, a box of mathematical instruments, a quantity (400) cartridges, a large box of photographic plates and negatives, three bags. We did not molest any one, and paid more than four times the value for any food we bought.

Read over to witness.

J. LARKIN.

DEPOSITION OF MAN SING, *taken on the 9th day of October, 1897. Solemn affirmation administered by Pandit Krishnanand.*

My name is Man Sing; my father's name is Sohan Sing; I am by caste Pharswal; twenty-five years of age; by occupation *khati*; my home is at Sileri, police station Bichla Kattyur, district Almora.

I accompanied Mr. Savage Landor into Thibet. We were surrounded and arrested at Toxem while bargaining and selecting ponies. I was tied up hand and foot, and again tied to a

APPENDIX

log of wood with my master. When I begged for mercy, they
threatened to behead me and struck me on the head with the
handle of a *kukri*. We were taken to Galshio. There the Thibetans were on the point of beheading my master. They tried
to burn out his eyes. They fired at him twice to kill him. They
tried to pull him off his horse to have him trampled upon. He
was subjected to many insults and hardships. We were kept
bound and guarded until brought to Mansarowar. There our
hands were untied. Chanden Sing was with us. He received
about two to three hundred lashes at Toxem. I got off most light-
ly, as when the three of us were captured and examined, I said
I was merely the yak driver, and not responsible for anything.
I lost nothing, but they took my master's property—three firearms, some money, and other things ; I cannot enumerate them.
We were brought back to Taklakot, where we met friends. My
master was made to sit on a spiked saddle and taken from Toxem
to Galshio.

Read over to witness.

J. LARKIN.

DEPOSITION OF THE REV. HARKUA WILSON, *taken on the 9th
day of October, 1897. Oath administered by me.*

My name is Harkua Wilson. By caste Christian ; forty - six
years of age ; by occupation missionary ; my home is at Dwara-
hat, police station M. Dwara, district Almora. I reside at Gunji,
Byans.

I am a missionary in the American Methodist Episcopal Society.
My work is in the northern *pattis* or Bhot. I accompanied Mr.
Savage Landor in July last as far as Gyanima in Thibet. We
went through the Lumpia Pass. It took us four days from
Lumpiya to get to Gyanima. At this place the Barkha Tarjam
declined to allow me to go on, but he allowed Mr. Landor (who
was said to be my brother) with four porters and three servants
to go on ; but the following day he withdrew this permission.
We then returned three marches. At midnight in a snow-storm
Mr. Landor went up the mountains, determining to go through
Thibet by the wilds. He had with him nine followers. He

231

was then in perfect health and strength, and so were his followers. At the end of August I heard that Mr. Landor had been arrested, and, fearing the Thibetans would kill him, I hastened to Taklakot to do my utmost to save him. There I learnt that Mr. Landor and his two servants were being brought back. Hearing that it was the intention of the Thibetans to take them *via* the Lumpia, I, with Pandit Gobaria, Jai Mal, and Lata, induced the Jong Pen of Taklakot to allow Mr. Landor to be brought to Taklakot. On the evening of 7th September *Peshkar* Kharak Sing arrived there. At about 11 A.M. on the 8th September Mr. Landor, Chanden Sing, and Man Sing arrived. I took them to my tent and heard their account of what had happened. I could hardly recognize Mr. Landor; he looked very ill and seemed nearly exhausted. I examined his injuries and found that his forehead had the skin off and was covered with scabs. His cheeks and nose were in the same state. His hair had grown long. He was unshaven and unkempt. He was in rags and dirty, covered with swarms of lice. His hands, fingers, and wrists were swollen and wounded. On his spine at the waist he had an open sore, and the parts around were swollen and red. His seat was covered with marks of wounds caused by spikes. His feet were swollen, and so were his ankles. The flesh about the latter was much hurt and contused, showing marks of cords having been tightly bound round them. He was in a very low condition. I attended to him, having given him a bath and a change of clothes. I gave him food, but though he said he was famished, he could scarcely eat. I am confident, if he had been a few days longer in the hands of the Thibetans and had been taken *via* Lumpia, he would have died. After half an hour the Thibetans brought some of Mr. Landor's things under seal. Some of the Thibetan officials on one side, *Peshkar* Kharak Sing and Gobaria and myself on the other, made out a list of the property, which we took over, and a list was prepared of the articles taken from Mr. Landor and which were missing. Mr. Landor dictated the list from memory. Copies of these lists were furnished to the Jong Pen. I kept Mr. Landor at Taklakot until the afternoon of the 11th September. Then I conveyed him by easy stages to Gunji, where I have a dispensary, and attended to him. I am a hospital assistant. I sent off reports to the Commissioner and Deputy Commissioner. Chanden Sing and Man Sing were also in a wretched state. The former had marks of recent flogging from his waist to above his ankles.

Read over to witness.

J. LARKIN.

DEPOSITION OF PANDIT GOBARIA, *taken on the 13th day of October, 1897. Solemn affirmation administered by Pandit Krishnanand.*

My name is Gobaria; my father's name is Jaibania; I am by caste Garbial; forty-eight years of age; by occupation trader; my home is at Garbyang, police station Byans, district Almora.

I heard that Mr. Landor had been arrested and brought down as far as Rungu, and saw that the Jong Pen of Taklakot was sending men to divert Mr. Landor by the long roundabout route *via* the Lumpia Pass. I went to the Jong Pen and succeeded in getting him to allow Mr. Landor to be brought to Taklakot. Next morning Mr. Landor and his two servants with two yaks arrived. Mr. Landor was in a very bad state —in a dying state. A list of Mr. Landor's property as received from the Tokchim Tarjum was made. Then Mr. Landor had a list of things taken from him and not returned made out. A Thibetan named Nerba, who was present, admitted that he had taken part in Mr. Landor's torture and had held him by the hair. The official who had tortured Mr. Landor was the Galjo Changjo and a Lama.

Read over to witness.

J. LARKIN.

DEPOSITION OF THE POLITICAL PESHKÁR KHARAK SING, *taken on the 9th day of October, 1897. Solemn affirmation administered by me.*

My name is Kharak Sing; my father's name is Gobind Sing; I am by caste Pal; twenty-six years of age; by occupation *Peshkár;* my home is at Askot, police station Askot, district Almora.

I am the Political *Peshkar* at Garbyang in Byans. I knew and reported that Mr. Henry Savage Landor had gone into Thibet. On the 5th September I learnt from Bhotias that he had been stopped at Toxem, and reported it. I then proceeded to Taklakot, in Thibet, to inquire into the matter. On the 7th September, at Taklakot, I learnt that Mr. Landor was a prisoner at Dogmar, and that the Jong Pen would not permit his being brought into Taklakot, as this meant that Mr. Landor would have to go to Gyanima and *via* the Lumpia Lek. I then insisted on the Jong Pen allowing Mr. Landor a passage to Taklakot, and warned him of the consequences if he declined. The Jong Pen consented, but gave orders that Mr. Landor should be conveyed hurriedly by night through Taklakot to the Lippu Lek. I protested against this, and eventually Mr. Landor, on 8th September, was conveyed into Taklakot. The Jong Pen had sent two *sawars* to his guard to admit them. In the Rev. Harkua Wilson's tent Mr. Landor related how he had been tortured. There were several of the Thibetans present who had taken part in the tortures, and they signified that all of Mr. Landor's story was true. Among them was Nerba, of Thokchim Tarjum, who admitted that he had held Mr. Landor by the hair when about to be beheaded, and had cut the nails of his fingers and toes. He admitted he had taken a gold ring from Mr. Landor, which a soldier had taken from him. I made a report of all this and sent (1) a list of Mr. Landor's property restored him by the Thibetans and (2) a list of articles missing. I know Mr. Landor had two rifles and a revolver when he went into Thibet and a considerable amount of money. Mr. Landor was in a very critical position; he was past recognition. He was wounded on the face, body, hands, and legs. I went to the Jong Pen and protested at the treatment given Mr. Landor. The former boldly admitted that Mr. Landor had been treated as alleged, and that it was their duty to act so. The Jong Pen promised to try and have Mr. Landor's missing property restored to him. I know he wrote off to the Garban of Gartok about orders issuing to the Toxem Tarjum. He has engaged to send me anything recovered.

Read over to witness.
                                        J. LARKIN.

APPENDIX

DEPOSITION OF SUNA, *taken on the 14th day of October, 1897. Solemn affirmation administered by me.*

My name is Suna; my father's name is Gandachiju; I am by caste Khumhar; forty-two years of age; by occupation trader; my home is at Gunji, police station Byans, district Almora.

I saw Mr. Landor and his two servants as prisoners about one and a half month ago, this side of the Mansarowar Lake. Mr. Landor and Chanden Sing were on yaks; Man Sing on foot. They were well guarded. Tunda and Amr Sing were with me. They went on ahead to Taklakot while I stayed back with the sheep. They went to inform the Rev. Harkua Wilson of the capture. I saw Mr. Landor detained at Dogmar.

Read over to witness.   J. LARKIN.

H.—T

Statement of property confiscated by the Tibetan authorities, and recovered some months later by the Government of India.

189

DEPARTMENT

From

H. K. GRACEY, Esq., C.S.,
The Deputy Commissioner of Almora,

To

A. H. SAVAGE LANDOR, Esq.,
c/o GRINDLAY, GROOM & CO.
BOMBAY.

Dated 10th December
Received } 1897

807
No. XXII. of 1897.

File No. .

Serial No. .

Revolver, 1.
Jewel ring, 1.
Cash — 68/12/ — in eight-anna
    pieces.
Cartridges for rifles, 110.
Rifles, 2 (1 damaged).
Cartridges for pistol, 37.
Cleaning-rods for rifles, 2.
Cover for rifle, 1.
    "   revolver, 1.
Leather strap, 1.
Net to catch butterflies, 1.

File Heading.
Property of Mr. H. SAVAGE
LANDOR.

SUBJECT.

Has the honour to inform him
that his marginally noted articles have been received by the
Political Peshkar of Garbiang
from the Jong-pong of Takla-
kote.

W. SMITH, C.S., *for*
H. K. GRACEY, C.S.,
Deputy Commissioner, Almora.
W. J. W.

B. R. Regr. No. 27 } P. No. 2131
Dept. XXII. B.--- } 11 9 96-
1,00,000 of 1896. } P. D.

APPENDIX

Certificate from DR. WILSON.

DHARCHULA BYAS, BHOT.

I herewith certify that I accompanied Mr. A. Henry Savage Landor in his ascent up the Mangshan Mountain, and that Mr. Landor and a Rongba coolie reached an altitude of 22,000 (twenty-two thousand) feet. Owing to the rarefied air, I and the other men accompanying Mr. Landor were unable to go as far as he did. Mr. Landor was at the time carrying on him a weight of thirty seers (60 lbs.), consisting of silver rupees, two aneroids, cartridges, revolver, &c. During the whole time I travelled with Mr. Landor he always carried the above weight on him, and generally carried his rifle besides (7½ lbs. extra). We all suffered very much during the ascent, as the incline was very steep, and there was deep snow and much troublesome débris.

I also certify that I took many photographs* of Mr. Landor and his two servants after they were released, and Mr. Landor looked then very old and suffering, owing to starvation and the wounds that had been inflicted upon him by the Tibetans.

(Signed). H. WILSON,
In charge of Bhot Dispensaries,
American Methodist Episcopal Mission.

DHARCHULA, *April* 27, 1898.

DEAR MR. LANDOR:

Do you remember the night when we separated near Lama Chokden in Tibet, you to proceed towards Lhassa, and I to return to India?

I have in my lifetime seen few such fierce snow-storms. The storm had been raging the whole day and night, and the wind was blowing so hard that we could not hear each other speak. I can only recollect with horror at the dreadful anxiety I was in when you, with a handful of men, escaped from the Tibetan soldiers watching us, and in the dark, fearful night proceeded to take your men up the mountain range, with no path, and among loose stones and boulders, a way, indeed, not even fit for goats.

---

* N.B.—Reproductions of some of the photographs mentioned are given in this book.

That night, I well remember, you were carrying a weight much greater than the one you usually carried, thirty seers (60 lbs.), for when you left the tent you had in your hand a small bag with 200 extra silver rupees, and you carried your revolver, your rifle, and some extra ammunition. I assure you that I look back with amazement at how you succeeded in pulling through the dangers and difficulties of that night alone.

Yours sincerely,

(Signed) H. WILSON.

American Methodist Episcopal Mission.

DR. H. WILSON'S *Statement.*

I herewith certify that, having heard at Gungi (Byas) that Mr. A. Henry Savage Landor, after losing all his provisions in a large river, had been captured by the Tibetans at Toxem and had there been tortured, I proceeded to Taklakot (Tibet) in the hope of obtaining further news. At Taklakot the news was confirmed, and I heard that Mr. Landor and two servants were brought back under a strong guard. Some uncertainty prevailed as to what route he would be made to follow, and efforts were made by the Tibetans to make him proceed by the long, cold, and dangerous route *via* the Lumpiya Pass, instead of by the shorter and easier route *via* Taklakot. We heard that Mr. Landor and his two men were in very poor health owing to the ill treatment by the Tibetans, and no doubt the long journey over ice and snow by the Lumpiya Pass left but little chance of their reaching Gungi alive. At the request of Jaimal Bura, Latto Bura, and myself, Pundit Gobaria despatched a man to the Jong Pen at Kujer to explain that we would be thankful and would consider it a great kindness if he would allow Mr. Landor to travel through Taklakot. At last, after much trouble, our request was granted. The officer who brought us the news informed us that Mr. Landor would be made to pass through Taklakot at night, and conveyed directly over the Lippu Pass. The Political Peshkar Kharak Sing Pal arrived in Taklakot that day from India, and we held a consultation. We agreed to keep a watchman in the road all night, but Mr. Landor did not go by. In the afternoon of the 8th, Mr. Landor and his two men arrived. They had been rifled of all they possessed and their clothes were torn and dirty. Mr. Landor and the two men looked very ill and suffering, Mr. Landor's face being hardly recognizable. He and his bearer Chanden Sing gave us an account of the tortures that had been inflicted upon them at Toxem and Galshio, and Mr. Landor showed the Peshkar Kharak Singh, Pundit Gobaria, myself and many Bhotiyas (Shokas) twenty-two wounds on his spine, feet, and hands received from the Tibetans. Chanden Sing, who had been administered two hundred lashes, showed numerous black marks and open sores where the skin had been torn on both legs. From the Lamas and soldiers who had been present at Mr. Landor's arrest and tortures I heard the following account.

An ambush had been laid, and Mr. Landor and his bearer were caught by treachery when some hundred and fifty yards away from their tent, inside which were the rifles and revolver. They made a desperate resistance and fought for over fifteen minutes, struggling to get at their weapons. Thirty men were on Mr. Landor and twelve or fifteen held Chanden Sing, while four hundred soldiers armed with matchlocks and swords, and who had kept hidden behind sand-hills, quickly surrounded them. They were tightly bound with ropes round the neck, chest, and legs, and the arms were pinioned behind their backs. Chanden Sing received two hundred lashes that same day. Mr. Landor and Mansing were taken to Galshio three days later. Ponies were provided for them, Mansing riding bareback, while the wooden frame of a saddle was provided for Mr. Landor, the frame having several iron spikes sticking out of it in the back part of it. During the long ride to Galshio these nails produced several wounds on Mr. Landor's spine and back. Efforts were made, by means of a rope attached to his handcuffs, to pull him off the saddle and have him trodden to death by the hundreds of ponies of the Lamas, soldiers, and officers that came full-gallop behind. Moreover, two shots were fired at Mr. Landor. Mansing, unable to use his hands, that were bound, fell many times off his steed and remained some two miles behind. When Galshio was reached Mr. Landor was pulled off his saddle, and they told him that his head would be cut off immediately. Dragged mercilessly by soldiers, he was taken to a wooden log. Here they stretched his legs wide apart, and his feet were made fast on the cutting edge of the log by means of tightly bound ropes that cut into his flesh. Then while an officer held him in a standing position by the hair of his head, a hot iron was passed in front of his eyes and a matchlock laid on his forehead and fired. Lastly, the head Lama approached with a long sword and swung it right and left close to Mr. Landor's neck, as if about to cut off the head. Mr. Landor remained composed and spoke no words. After some twenty minutes Mansing arrived, and was tied to the same log in front of Mr. Landor, and pretence was made to behead Mansing, Mr. Landor's face having been covered with a cloth. The Lamas professed to have been very astonished when, after having tied the prisoners' hands high up to poles behind them, Mr. Landor asked for some *tsamba* (oatmeal), meat, and rice, and Mansing for some butter.

The amazement of the Tibetans appears to have been even greater when food was brought and Mr. Landor and Mansing partook heartily of it and asked for more. Mr. Landor was kept chained to the log for twenty-four hours, Mansing twelve hours. When they were brought back to Toxem they found that Chanden Sing had been kept four days tied hands and feet to an upright post, and he had been given no food.

At Taklakot an officer (called Nerba) confessed in my own tent, and before Pundit Gobaria and the Political Peshkar Kharak Sing, that he himself had held Mr. Landor by the hair when he was about to be beheaded. He had also fired a shot at Mr. Landor, and had moreover been ordered by the Lamas to cut off Mr. Landor's toe and finger nails, as well as a lock of his hair. The Taklakot Lamas and the Tokchim Tarjum professed to be sorry at the Galshio Lamas having behaved in such a cruel manner.

At Taklakot we made a list of Mr. Landor's property that was still missing, and we gave a copy to the Jong Pen and one to the Tokchim Tarjum, that they may try to recover what they can.

(Signed) HARKUA WILSON,
Methodist Episcopal Mission.

GUNGI BYAS BHOT, DARMA. *Sept.* 21. 1897.

APPENDIX

Dr. H. Wilson's *Certificate of* A. Henry Savage Landor's *injuries and wounds.*

Taklakot, Tibet, *Sept.* 8, 1897.

I herewith certify that I have examined the wounds that Mr. A. Henry Savage Landor received during his imprisonment at Galshio in Tibet.

There are five large sores along the spinal column, and the spine itself has sustained severe injuries. At the time they were inflicted these wounds must have caused profuse bleeding.

The feet bear the marks of cruel treatment. On the right foot are still well visible to-day (nineteen days after wounds were inflicted) six wounds, viz.:

On the heel one wound one inch long;
Outside ankle   "   half inch long;
Front of ankle   "   one inch long;
Top of foot, three inches above the toes, one wound one and a half inch long.
Two small wounds on the upper part of foot.

On the left foot the four wounds are of a very severe character, and were produced by ropes cutting into the flesh.
One nasty wound above heel, two and a half inches long.
One wound below the ankle, one and one-fourth of an inch long.
One wound three inches above the toes, two inches long.
One   "   on the heel, half an inch long.

These wounds have caused the feet to be much swollen, the left foot especially having been considerably injured. Its strained tendons give still intense pain when touched, and the foot is very heavy, inflamed, and swollen.

On the left hand there are five wounds.
On middle finger a wound one inch long and deep to the bone.
On root of middle finger, a wound half an inch long.

On small finger a wound one-fourth of an inch long.

On third　　　"　　　　　"　　　　"　　　　"

On first　　　"　　　　　"　　half an inch long.

The four fingers are still very swollen.

On the right hand there are only two wounds.

The first, one-half inch long, on the upper side of the hand.

The second, a quarter of an inch long on the second finger.

Both hands are aching and much swollen, and the wounds upon them were evidently produced by the heavy iron chain of the handcuffs.

On arrival at Taklakot (nineteen days after having been tortured) Mr. Landor is still suffering from strong fever caused by his wounds, and no doubt when they were fresh these must have given Mr. Landor intense pain. His health and strong constitution seem altogether shattered by the sufferings he has undergone.

His face, hands, and feet are very swollen, and he appears extremely weak; he himself attributed his great exhaustion to having been unable to sleep for nineteen consecutive nights on account of the bad sores on the spine and legs and because of the heavy iron chains with which he was laden.

H. WILSON,

Hospital Assistant, Methodist Episcopal Mission.

GUNGE BYAS BHOT, DARMA.

N. B.—The numerous smaller wounds, burns, &c., on the face and body are not taken into account.

A copy of this report was despatched from Dr. Wilson direct to the Deputy Commissioner, and was forwarded to the Government of India.

DR. H. WILSON'S *Certificate of* CHANDEN SING'S *injuries.*

TAKLAKOT, *Sept. 8, 1897.*

I herewith certify that I have examined Chanden Sing, Mr. A. Henry Savage Landor's servant who accompanied him to Tibet, where they were arrested and tortured. Chanden Sing has visible to this day on both his legs, and twenty-one days after they were inflicted, innumerable black marks produced by flogging. So severely appears the punishment to have been administered that large patches of skin and flesh have been torn off by the lashing. Chanden Sing is now in very poor health, and it is evident by his appearance that he suffers greatly from the tortures and ill-treatment received at the hands of the Tibetans.

H. WILSON,

Hospital Assistant, Methodist Episcopal Mission.

GUNGI BYAS, BHOT, DARMA.

A copy of this was sent by Dr. Wilson to the Deputy Commissioner at Almora, and was forwarded to the Government of India.

Certificate by MISS M. A. SHELDON, M.D., *of the Methodist Episcopal Mission.*

M. E. MISSION,
   KHELA P. O. DIST. ALMORA.
EAST KUMAON, BHOT.

" All at it and always at it."—WESLEY.

Sept. 28, 1897.

This is to certify that I have seen the wounds inflicted upon Mr. Landor by the Tibetans. It is now about forty days since he was bound and tortured. The wounds are healing well. The scars upon his hands caused by being bound with chains behind his back are plainly visible.

The feet show even more clearly the results of inhuman binding and torture. The wounds have not yet entirely healed, and there is much discoloration. One foot is still swollen.

I have not seen the wounds upon his spine inflicted by a torturing saddle, but he complains of much pain and soreness in that region.

(Signed)   MARTHA A. SHELDON, M.D.

IN THE FORBIDDEN LAND

Certificate from DOCTOR TURCHINI, *a Director of the Royal Hospital of S. M. Nuova, Florence, Italy.*

D. D. | C. 50 |

Stamp

R. ARCISPEDALE DI S. M. NUOVA,
GABINETTO
ELETTRO-TERAPICO
DIREZIONE,
FIRENZE.

FIRENZE, 12 *Febbraio*, 1898.

Il sottoscritto Medico Primario Direttore del Turno e Gabinetto elettro-terapico del R° Arcispedale di S. Maria Nuova dichiara quanto appresso: nel mese di Dicembre appena giunto in questa Città visitò il Sig° Henry Savage Landor e lo trovò affeto =

Da *retinite* all' occhio sinistro con suffusione dei mezzi trasparenti, e *da grave iperemia retinica* all' occhio destro. La vista era *abolita* a sinistra, *diminuita* a destra =

La *colonna vertebrale* era dolente, se leggermente compressa con un dito, o se appena percossa col martello da percussione il dolore si faceva intenso, acuto specialmente nelle regioni lombare e dorsale. La deambulazione non era libera ma incerta, la funzionalità degli sfinteri molto difettosa per cui difficolta della mizione e delle evacuazioni.

Presentava poi delle chiazze ecchimobili sopra-malleolari e sopra-carpiche. L'aspetto suo generale era di persona sofferente e molto anemica. Fatte le cure che il caso del Sig° Landor reclamava, oggi 12 Febbraio notiamo: all' occhio destro risoluta la iperemia retinica, aumentato il campo visivo, occhio che serve discretamente alla sua funzione; all' occhio sinistro è molto turbata la circolazione endoculare e quivi la funzione visiva non è ristabilita; non vede gli oggetti e tutto gli fa confusione. La colonna vertebrale presenta sempre dei punti dolenti in specie al rigonfiamento sacro lombare. La deambulazione è più corretta, ma le sarebbe impossibile fare una passeg-

APPENDIX

giata lunga. La mizione e megliorata, non così la defacazione
che è sempre difettosa per impotenza dello sfintere.

Le condizioni generali sono megliorate, ma occorre però al
Sig.^{re} Landor seguire la cura intrapresa, e specialmente la cura
elettrica ed idroterapica.

(Signed)   DOTT. TURCHINI.

COMUNE DI FIRENZE.
OFFICIO D'IGIENE,

*Visto per la legalizzazione della
firma del Sig. Dott. Turchini.
Dal Municipio Firenze
Li 12 Febbraio 1898.*

1 *Lira Stamp.*
Il Sindaco.
P. I.
A. Artimini.

Letter from the POLITICAL PESHKAR, KHARAK SING.

Private.

GARBYANG, BHOT,
November 13, 1897.

MY DEAR MR. LANDOR :

I hope that you have received my letter of some time ago
and that you may be quite well now. Are you still at Almora?
I have not yet got back your things from the Jong Pen, but I
hear it is quite true that all your property reached Tokchim a
long time ago. I have sent another letter to the Jong Pen, but
cannot get an answer, as the Lippu Pass is now closed, owing
to a heavy fall of snow yesterday. It is rumored that a Tibetan
officer is coming from Lhassa to Taklakot to inquire after your
case, and probably he may have reached Taklakot yesterday,
and after examining your things he will send them down to me.
Now I have nearly finished my work at this place. I have collected the dues and paid them to the agents of the Jong Pen.
I will go back to Chaudas the day after to-morrow—*i.e.*, on the
15th of this month.

With kind regards, and hoping to hear from you soon.
I remain,
Yours sincerely,
KHARAK SING PAL.

IN THE FORBIDDEN LAND

Letter from the POLITICAL PESHKAR, KHARAK SING PAL.

HALDWANI, *January* 11, 1898.

MY DEAR MR. LANDOR:

I hope that by this time you have reached safely home. I have been very anxious, as I have not heard from you or of your safe arrival there. The dreadful day of the 8th of September is still vivid in my mind, when I first saw you at Taklakot (in Tibet) after you had been tortured by the Tibetans, and where I had come in search of you.

I cannot forget your fearful appearance, with long hair and beard, and your face, body, and limbs covered with wounds and bruises. When you arrived at Taklakot, in a few miserable rags stained with blood, dirty and swarming with lice, and surrounded by the guard of Tibetans, I could hardly believe it possible that it was you who stood before me, so much you had changed since I had last seen you.

I am still deeply pained when I think of the pitiable condition you were in, when you showed me 22 (twenty-two) fresh wounds on your hands, feet, and spine, without counting the injuries to your face. And indescribable pain gave us too seeing your confiscated baggage under seal of the Tibetan authorities, and to find, when we opened it, to be full of broken or damaged instruments and other articles of your property.

I think that you may remember my enquiry and consequent anger when the Tibetan officers and soldiers admitted their guilt of tying you by your limbs to the stretching log and of placing you on a spiked saddle; of removing forcibly your toe-nails and pulling you by the hair of your head. You know quite well that I had no power to do more than to report the matter to higher authorities, but I can assure you that it was to me quite unbearable to hear from the Tibetans that they had brought you to execution, and that they boasted of having swung the naked executioner's sword right and left of your neck, and that they had brought a red-hot iron close to your eyes to blind you.

Your servants' condition, especially that of Chanden Sing, whom like yourself the Tibetans kept prisoner for twenty-four days, and who was given two hundred lashes, was pitiable beyond words.

APPENDIX

I am anxious to see the photographs taken by Dr. Wilson of you as you were when you arrived at Taklakot. I trust that by now you may feel better, and that the pain in your spine may have altogether disappeared. I believe your rifles, revolver, ring, &c., which I succeeded in recovering from the Tibetans, must have reached you by now through the Deputy Commissioner at Almora. The cash and other articles have not been recovered, nor is there any probability of getting them back. Hoping to receive news of you soon, and with best salaams,

I am, yours most obediently,

K. KHARAK SING PAL,
Political Peshkar,
Garbyang Dharchula, Bhot.

Letter from COLONEL GRIGG, *Commissioner of Kumaon.*

Commissionership of Kumaon.
Dated December 7, 1897.

MY DEAR LANDOR:

Karak Sing reports that 2 guns (1 damaged), 1 revolver, 1 signet-ring, cash 68/12/-, cartridges (gun) 110, ditto revolver 37, cleaning-rods 2, gun-case 1, leather straps, 1 butterfly-catcher, &c., have been handed to him by the Jong Pen of Taklakot, and he has requested Deputy Commissioner's orders.

I am glad to hear your things are coming on. I hope you are getting stronger.

With our kindest regards,

Yours very sincerely,

E. E. GRIGG.

IN THE FORBIDDEN LAND

[Note by the Author.—*This letter, as will be seen from the date, reached me after the bulk only of the book had gone to press.*]

A PRIVATE LETTER FROM J. LARKIN, Esq., WHO, DEPUTED BY THE GOVERNMENT, PROCEEDED TO THE FRONTIER TO MAKE AN INQUIRY INTO MY CASE.

ALMORA, *August* 10, 1898.

MY DEAR LANDOR:

Yours of the 21st ult. I am glad to hear that your book on your experiences in Tibet is nearly finished. I wish you may have every success with it, as it is only what you deserve after your trials and hardships in that difficult land of the ultra-conservative Lamas. I am not aware that the Indian papers are attacking you. However, they apparently do not get reliable information if they dispute the fact of your having entered Tibet. We who were in some way connected with your rescue and return have not been "interviewed," or we would give the authentic account of the affair.

I was on a few days' leave at Naini Tal when I heard of your capture, tortures, and expulsion from Tibet. I was deputed by the Government to proceed at once to the borders and make an inquiry into the affair. I set off at once, and I met you at Askot, where you were being looked after by the Rajbar. What a change in your appearance! When I saw you standing among some of the Askot natives I could with difficulty identify you. You were bronzed and weather-beaten to such an extent that you were not distinguishable from the natives. I do not think you can blame me for not recognizing you readily. Your forehead, nose, and the part of your face below your eyes were scarred, and helped to alter your appearance very greatly. You did surprise me when you told me that you would retrace your steps back to the borders on learning from me that I was hastening on to inquire into your case. I had then seen the twenty odd wounds you had on your face, wrists, feet, and back. I strongly protested against your undertaking the fatiguing journey back across the perilous and arduous road, as I knew you needed rest and good nourishment, and thought it would be wisest for you to get back to Almora, and be under a good doctor.

You, however, with your characteristic doggedness, meant to accompany me, and I must perforce let you. I was glad in the long run, for you enabled me to make a fuller inquiry than I would otherwise have been able.

As you know, and as I reported to Government, I found after an inquiry on the borders that you had with great difficulty and manœuvring succeeded in entering Tibet, evading the Jong Pen of Taklakot, and the Barca Tarjum at Gyanema, and crossing the Mariam La (Maium Pass) and getting as far as Tuksem (Toxem). You had been deserted by all the mountaineers who had started with you and who had promised to accompany you wherever you went. When you were left with the two Kumaonis, you were surrounded and captured by the *Governor of that part of Tibet* and his men. There, as a sequel to your innumerable fatigues, hardships, desertions, and privations, you and your two followers were ill-treated and tortured *by the Governor*. Have you not got a copy of my official report? I remember you told me you were applying for it. If you possess the copy, surely that will be sufficient to confound your traducers. I saw from the public papers that my report was to be laid on the table of the House of Commons by the Secretary of State for India.

How did the photographs which we took up at the Lippu Pass turn out? I should particularly like to have the one of the group on the pass, and also the one where I am on horseback. I would also like to have the one *I took of you having your matutinal bath when the water froze in your hair and on your body* as it was thrown on you by Chanden Sing; and no wonder it did, as there was ten to twelve feet of snow lying about, and a hardy Bhotia (Shoka) mountaineer had only a few days prior to our arrival been lost in the snow on crossing the pass.

Doubtless it will afford you some pleasure to learn that you have earned quite a reputation among the natives, both Tibetan and Bhotias (Shokas), on account of your universal cordiality, generosity, and pluck. They are constantly inquiring about you, and relating your many good traits. Should you ever think of returning here you have made many friends, and you would get a very warm welcome from the natives.

Dr. H. Wilson tells me that, when he took you over from your captors, *the officials of Tibet*, you were in a dying state, and that he only just got you in the nick of time. How are your eyes and spine? I trust they are quite well again. I look back with pleasure to my tour up to the border with you, and our return journey after your journey into Tibet proper, *where you were subjected to tortures by the Governor of the district thereof.*

With every good wish,

Yours very sincerely,

(Signed) J. LARKIN.

www.ingramcontent.com/pod-product-compliance
Lightning Source LLC
Chambersburg PA
CBHW021213270326
41929CB00010B/1104